CARTAGENA TRAVEL GUIDE

The Complete Guide to the Must-See Attractions, Things to Do, Hotels, Itinerary, Beaches, Culture and Food of Columbia's Gem Everything to Know Before Planning Your Trip

CLARA CARTER

Copyright © 2024 by Clara Carter

All rights reserved. No part of this publication may be reproduced, distributed, or transmitted in any form or by any means, including photocopying, recording, or other electronic or mechanical methods, without the prior written permission of the publisher.

TABLE OF CONTENTS

INTRODUCTION.. 6
    About Cartagena:... 8
    Reasons to Love Cartagena... 10
    History and Culture Overview... 12

CHAPTER 1: PLANNING YOUR TRIP TO CARTAGENA 14
    When to Visit Cartagena.. 16
    How to Get to Cartagena... 17
    Getting Around Cartagena... 18
    Where to Stay: Neighbourhoods in Cartagena............................ 20
    What to Pack... 22
    Entry and Visa Requirements.. 24
    Currency and Language.. 26
    Suggested Budget.. 28
    Money-Saving Tips.. 30
    Best Places to Book Your Trip... 32

CHAPTER 2: MUST-SEE ATTRACTIONS AND LANDMARKS.. **34**
    Cartagena's Old Town... 36
    Castillo San Felipe de Barajas.. 38
    Rosario Islands... 40
    Cartagena's Walls.. 42
    Palacio de la Inquisición.. 44
    Convento de la Popa... 46
    Plaza Santo Domingo... 48
    San Pedro Claver Church... 50
    Bocagrande Beach.. 52
    Getsemaní Neighborhood.. 54
    La Boquilla Beach.. 56

    Clock Tower (Torre del Reloj)... 58
CHAPTER 3: ACCOMMODATION OPTIONS................ 60
    Best Luxury Hotels and Resorts... 62
    Budget-Friendly Accommodations.. 64
    Unique Stays and Local Favorites.. 66
    Tips for Choosing the Perfect Accommodation..................... 68
CHAPTER 4: DINING AND CUISINE........................ 70
    Best Restaurants and Eateries..72
    Must-Try Local Delicacies... 74
    Dining with a View... 76
    Dining Etiquette and Local Foodie Tips................................78
CHAPTER 5: THINGS TO DO AND OUTDOOR ACTIVITIES... 80
    Snorkeling and Water Sports... 82
    Exploring the Mangroves... 84
    Beach Bliss... 86
    Hiking Adventures..88
    Outdoor Adventure Tips and Essentials............................... 90
CHAPTER 6: ART, CULTURE, AND ENTERTAINMENT... 92
    Local Arts and Crafts.. 94
    Museums and Galleries... 96
    Festivals and Events... 98
    Nightlife and Entertainment.. 100
    Local Markets, Shopping, and Souvenirs............................ 102
CHAPTER 7: 7-DAY ITINERARY IN CARTAGENA..... 104
    Day 1: Arrival and Old Town Exploration............................ 104
    Day 2: Rosario Islands Escape...105
    Day 3: Cultural Immersion in Getsemaní.............................105
    Day 4: Explore La Popa and San Felipe............................... 106
    Day 5: Beach Day in La Boquilla...107

Day 6: Art and Shopping Extravaganza.................107
Day 7: Relaxing Day and Farewell........................108
CHAPTER 8: PRACTICAL INFORMATION AND TIPS..... 109
Etiquette and Customs..109
Language and Communication................................111
Simple Language Phrases to Know........................ 113
Health and Safety Tips... 116
Emergency Contacts... 119
Communication and Internet Access................... 121
Useful Apps, Websites, and Maps..........................124
CONCLUSION.. 127

INTRODUCTION

Hello, dear traveler! As you flip through the pages of this travel guide, get ready to embark on a journey that goes beyond just a visit. I want to share with you my own memorable experience in Cartagena, a city that weaves history, culture, and a touch of magic into every corner.

The moment I stepped into the Old Town, the cobblestone streets whispered tales of a bygone era. The vibrant facades of colonial buildings stood as silent witnesses to centuries of stories. It was like walking through a living museum, where each turn brought me face-to-face with the city's rich history.

One highlight that etched itself into my memory was the imposing Castillo San Felipe de Barajas. The fortress, standing proudly against the Caribbean sky, offered a breathtaking panorama of the city. Climbing its ancient steps felt like a journey back in time, connecting me to the resilience of Cartagena's past.

The evenings in Cartagena are a celebration of life, and nowhere is this more evident than at Café Havana. The rhythmic beats of salsa music filled the air as locals and visitors alike danced under the starlit sky. It was here that I truly felt the heartbeat of the city, a pulsating energy that invited everyone to join the lively dance.

Exploring the local cuisine became a delightful adventure. La Cevicheria, with its fresh seafood dishes, became my go-to spot. Each bite was a burst of flavors, a testament to Cartagena's coastal heritage. Dining in the open air, surrounded by the sounds of the city, created an experience that transcended mere meals.

A day trip to the Rosario Islands added a touch of paradise to my Cartagena adventure. White sandy beaches, crystal-clear waters, and the warmth of the Caribbean sun made it a perfect escape. Snorkeling in the vibrant coral reefs felt like exploring an underwater wonderland.

As I strolled through the Centro de Artesanias, shopping for emeralds, I realized that Cartagena wasn't just a destination; it was an emotion. Each piece of jewelry became a tangible memory, a keepsake from a city that had captured my heart.

So, as you dive into the details of this guide, envision yourself walking the same cobblestone streets, savoring the flavors, and dancing under the stars. Let my memorable experience in Cartagena be your guide, and may your journey be filled with the same magic that made my time in this city unforgettable. Your adventure awaits!

About Cartagena:

Nestled on the northern coast of Colombia, along the shores of the Caribbean Sea, Cartagena de Indias is not just a city; it's a living testament to centuries of rich history and vibrant culture. Known as one of the major ports in the region, Cartagena's roots delve deep into the colonial era, where it stood as a pivotal link in the route to the West Indies.

Steeped in historical significance, Cartagena played a crucial role as a former Spanish colony. It served as a strategic port for exporting Bolivian silver to Spain and was a hub for the import of enslaved Africans. The city's defensibility against pirate attacks in the Caribbean further solidified its importance, creating a tapestry of stories that echo through its cobblestone streets.

Cartagena's strategic location between the Magdalena and Sinú Rivers not only made it a vital link in the commercial maritime routes but also granted easy access to the interior of New Granada. By the early 1540s, it had established itself as a key port for trade between Spain and its overseas empire, leaving an indelible mark on the city's identity.

In the present day, Cartagena stands as the capital of the Bolívar Department, a vibrant metropolis with a population of over 870,000. Its bustling metropolitan area is the sixth-largest urban space in Colombia, a dynamic blend of economic activities that range from maritime and petrochemical industries to the thriving tourism sector.

As you wander through the charming streets of Cartagena, every colonial building and lively plaza tells a story of resilience, trade, and cultural fusion. The city's allure goes beyond its historic past, seamlessly merging with modern charms. So, as you explore this guide, remember that Cartagena is not just a destination—it's an immersive experience that invites you to discover the layers of its captivating history and the vibrancy of its present. Welcome to Cartagena, where every corner is a chapter waiting to be explored.

Reasons to Love Cartagena

Welcome to a city that captures hearts effortlessly, where every street whispers tales of history, and the air is filled with the rhythm of life. Cartagena, with its unique blend of charm and vibrancy, has a way of leaving an indelible mark on those who wander its cobblestone streets. Here are some compelling reasons why we fell head over heels for this enchanting destination:

Historical Tapestry: Cartagena is a living museum, where each colonial building and fortress stands as a testament to a bygone era. The echoes of its past, from the days of Bolivian silver trade to the challenges of pirate attacks, create a captivating historical tapestry that unfolds with every step.

Culinary Delights: The local cuisine is a celebration of flavors that dance on the taste buds. From the fresh seafood at La Cevicheria to the street food adventures that beckon at every corner, Cartagena's culinary scene is a delightful journey for the senses.

Salsa Under the Stars: The lively beats of salsa music at Café Havana create an electrifying atmosphere. Whether you're a seasoned dancer or just tapping your feet to the rhythm, Cartagena invites everyone to join the dance and experience the city's pulsating energy.

Caribbean Paradise: A day trip to the Rosario Islands is like stepping into a postcard-perfect Caribbean paradise. White sandy beaches, crystal-clear waters, and the warm embrace of the sun make it a perfect escape from the hustle and bustle of everyday life.

Architectural Marvels: The architecture of Cartagena is a visual feast, blending colonial elegance with a touch of modern allure. From the iconic Baluarte Santo Domingo to the colorful facades of the Old Town, each building tells a story of Cartagena's aesthetic evolution.

Shopping for Emeralds: The Centro de Artesanias is a treasure trove for those seeking a piece of Colombia's signature gem—the emerald. Shopping for these precious stones becomes not just a transaction but a connection to the country's rich geological heritage.

Warm Hospitality: The people of Cartagena welcome visitors with open arms and warm smiles. Whether you're interacting with locals in the bustling markets or seeking guidance from friendly faces, the hospitality of Cartagena adds an extra layer of warmth to the overall experience.

As you explore Cartagena, let these reasons kindle your love for this captivating city. From its historical significance to the modern-day charms, Cartagena is a destination that invites you to fall in love over and over again.

History and Culture Overview

Cartagena de Indias, with its roots reaching deep into the pages of history, unfolds a captivating narrative that has shaped its identity over the centuries. The city was once a key port for exporting Bolivian silver to Spain, and its strategic location made it a linchpin in maritime exploration routes. As a former Spanish colony, Cartagena was not merely a city but a fortress defending against pirate attacks in the Caribbean, leaving an indelible mark on its historical landscape.

Wandering through the Old Town, one can't help but be transported back in time. The cobblestone streets echo with tales of resilience, trade, and cultural fusion. The architectural marvels, from the imposing Castillo San Felipe de Barajas to the colorful facades lining the plazas, narrate a story of colonial elegance evolving through the ages.

Cartagena's cultural heartbeat pulsates through its streets, and nowhere is this more evident than at Café Havana. The lively beats of salsa music, the infectious energy of locals and visitors dancing under the stars—it's a celebration of life that transcends time. The cultural immersion extends to the culinary scene, where the flavors of Cartagena's seafood and street food offerings become a journey for the taste buds.

In the present day, Cartagena stands as the capital of the Bolívar Department, a vibrant metropolis embracing its historical legacy while evolving into a modern hub. The city's economic activities, from maritime and petrochemical industries to the thriving tourism sector, showcase a harmonious blend of tradition and progress.

Cartagena's charm lies not just in its historical significance but in the way it seamlessly weaves its past into the fabric of the present. As you explore this city, every corner invites you to discover the layers of its captivating history and the vibrancy of its cultural tapestry—a tapestry that continues to unfold, telling the story of Cartagena's enduring allure.

CHAPTER 1: PLANNING YOUR TRIP TO CARTAGENA

Planning your unforgettable trip to Cartagena involves weaving together a tapestry of considerations that ensure a seamless and enriching experience. Begin by pondering the best time to visit this coastal gem. Cartagena's tropical climate is a crucial factor, with the dry season from December to March offering sun-soaked days and balmy evenings, ideal for exploring the city's vibrant streets and historical sites.

As you envision your journey, consider the various modes of reaching Cartagena. The Rafael Núñez International Airport serves as your gateway, and from there, whether you choose a taxi or a pre-arranged shuttle, the transition from arrival to immersion in Cartagena's charm is swift. Once in the city, navigating its enchanting streets becomes a joy, with options ranging from colorful local buses to easily accessible taxis, providing a hassle-free exploration of the Old Town and beyond.

Selecting the right neighborhood to stay in is pivotal to your Cartagena experience. Each area, from the historic Old Town to the lively Getsemani, boasts its own unique charm. As you contemplate your stay, consider the neighborhood's ambiance and proximity to must-see attractions, ensuring your accommodation enhances your overall adventure. Be sure to pack accordingly, embracing the tropical climate with light clothing, comfortable shoes, and, of course, sunscreen for those sunny escapades.

Before you embark, familiarize yourself with entry requirements, currency exchange, and language nuances. A smooth trip involves understanding the local currency, Colombian Pesos, and practicing a few basic Spanish phrases to enrich your interactions. Establishing a suggested budget and embracing money-saving tips can further enhance your experience, allowing you to savor Cartagena's offerings without unnecessary financial stress. Finally, explore reliable platforms to book your trip, ensuring a seamless journey from the moment you plan to the day you step into the captivating embrace of Cartagena.

When to Visit Cartagena

The best time to visit Cartagena largely depends on your preferences for weather and crowd levels. The city experiences a tropical climate with distinct wet and dry seasons.

The dry season, spanning from December to March, is considered the ideal time to visit Cartagena. During these months, rainfall is minimal, and the temperatures range from 75°F to 88°F (24°C to 31°C). The weather is sunny, offering pleasant conditions for exploring the city's historic sites, wandering through the cobblestone streets, and enjoying outdoor activities.

April to November constitutes the wet season, with increased rainfall and higher humidity. While temperatures remain relatively consistent, ranging from 75°F to 87°F (24°C to 31°C), there is a higher chance of rain. The peak of the wet season occurs from September to October, and it's advisable to consider this if you plan to visit during these months.

If you prefer a balance between fewer crowds and reasonable weather, the shoulder seasons of April to June and November to early December might be appealing. During these times, you can experience Cartagena with fewer tourists, allowing for a more intimate exploration of its rich history and vibrant culture.

Keep in mind that weather conditions can vary, so it's always a good idea to check the current forecasts closer to your travel dates to ensure a delightful and comfortable experience in Cartagena.

How to Get to Cartagena

Getting to Cartagena is a straightforward and exciting part of your journey. The primary point of entry is Rafael Núñez International Airport (CRA), conveniently located just 4 miles (7 kilometers) from the city center. The airport hosts a variety of domestic and international flights, connecting Cartagena to major cities across the Americas.

Upon arrival at Rafael Núñez International Airport, you have several transportation options to reach the heart of Cartagena. Taxis are readily available outside the terminal, providing a convenient and quick way to reach your accommodation. Alternatively, if you prefer a pre-arranged and often more cost-effective transfer, many hotels offer shuttle services, ensuring a smooth transition from the airport to your stay.

For those who enjoy a bit of adventure, public transportation is also an option. Local buses operate from the airport and can take you into different parts of the city. However, keep in mind that language barriers and the need for local currency might make this option more suitable for the seasoned traveler.

Navigating from the airport to your destination is a breeze, and soon after landing, you'll find yourself immersed in the vibrant energy of Cartagena. Whether it's the ease of a taxi ride or the anticipation of exploring the city by bus, getting to Cartagena sets the stage for an unforgettable experience in this enchanting destination.

Getting Around Cartagena

Getting around Cartagena is a delightful adventure, allowing you to explore the city's charming streets and vibrant neighborhoods with ease. The city offers various modes of transportation, catering to different preferences and budgets.

Local Buses: Cartagena has a network of colorful and affordable local buses, making them a popular choice for budget-conscious travelers. While the routes may take a bit of time to master, hopping on a local bus provides an authentic experience, allowing you to witness daily life in Cartagena.

Taxis: Taxis are a convenient and widely available option for getting around the city. They are recognizable by their yellow color, and you can either flag them down on the street or find them at designated taxi stands. Ensure the taxi has a meter, and it's advisable to confirm the fare before starting your journey.

Bicycle Rentals: Embrace a leisurely pace by renting a bicycle to navigate Cartagena. This eco-friendly option allows you to explore at your own rhythm, meandering through the historic Old Town or along the scenic coastline. Numerous rental shops offer a range of bicycles to suit your preferences.

Walking: Cartagena's Old Town is a pedestrian-friendly paradise. Exploring on foot allows you to soak in the city's atmosphere, discover hidden gems in narrow alleys, and stumble upon vibrant plazas. Comfortable shoes are a must for leisurely strolls through this enchanting area.

Boat Taxis: Given Cartagena's coastal location, boat taxis are a unique and enjoyable way to travel. They can take you to nearby islands, such as the Rosario Islands, offering a scenic journey over the turquoise waters of the Caribbean.

Whether you opt for the iconic local buses, the convenience of taxis, the leisure of bicycles, or the charm of walking, getting around Cartagena is an integral part of your experience, ensuring you don't miss a moment of this captivating city.

Where to Stay: Neighbourhoods in Cartagena

Choosing the right neighborhood to stay in Cartagena is a crucial decision that can shape your entire experience in this vibrant city. Each neighborhood possesses its own unique charm, catering to different preferences and interests.

Old Town (Ciudad Amurallada): The heart of Cartagena, the Old Town is a UNESCO World Heritage site adorned with colonial architecture, vibrant plazas, and historic landmarks. Staying here provides easy access to must-see attractions like Castillo San Felipe de Barajas and the iconic Plaza de Santo Domingo. The narrow cobblestone streets are lined with boutique hotels, charming guesthouses, and cozy cafes, creating an immersive atmosphere that transports you back in time.

Getsemani: Located just outside the Old Town, Getsemani is a bohemian neighborhood brimming with artistic flair and local character. Colorful street art, bustling markets, and a lively nightlife make Getsemani an ideal choice for those seeking a more eclectic and offbeat experience. The neighborhood offers a range of accommodation options, from budget-friendly hostels to boutique hotels, providing a taste of Cartagena's vibrant urban culture.

Bocagrande: If you prefer a more modern and cosmopolitan atmosphere, Bocagrande is a bustling area known for its upscale hotels, high-rise buildings, and a stretch of sandy beaches. This neighborhood offers a dynamic blend of shopping, dining, and entertainment, making it a great choice for those who enjoy a lively cityscape. The convenience of beachfront hotels and proximity to the Old Town adds to Bocagrande's appeal.

San Diego: Nestled between the Old Town and Getsemani, San Diego combines the historic charm of Cartagena with a more relaxed atmosphere. This area is known for its leafy plazas, stylish boutiques, and a mix of colonial and republican architecture. San Diego offers a range of accommodation options, from boutique hotels to charming bed and breakfasts, providing a tranquil yet central setting.

Whether you choose the timeless allure of the Old Town, the artistic energy of Getsemani, the cosmopolitan vibe of Bocagrande, or the peaceful charm of San Diego, your choice of neighborhood in Cartagena ensures a stay tailored to your preferences, creating the perfect backdrop for your exploration of this enchanting city.

What to Pack

Packing for your Cartagena adventure requires a thoughtful selection of items that cater to the city's tropical climate, vibrant culture, and varied activities. Here's a checklist to ensure you're well-prepared for your journey:

1. Light Clothing: Cartagena's weather is warm and tropical, so pack lightweight and breathable clothing. Think comfortable shorts, sundresses, and short-sleeved shirts to stay cool while exploring the city's vibrant streets.

2. Comfortable Shoes: With the charm of Cartagena lying in its cobblestone streets, comfortable walking shoes are essential. Sneakers or comfortable sandals are ideal for leisurely strolls through the Old Town.

3. Swimwear: Don't forget to pack your swimsuit! Whether you're enjoying the city's beaches or taking a boat trip to the nearby islands, having swimwear on hand ensures you're ready for a dip in the Caribbean Sea.

4. Sun Protection: The sun in Cartagena can be intense, so pack sunscreen, sunglasses, and a wide-brimmed hat to shield yourself from the sun's rays while exploring outdoor attractions.

5. Bug Repellent: While the city is not known for severe bug issues, it's always a good idea to have bug repellent, especially if you plan on venturing into more natural areas or during the evenings.

6. Lightweight Daypack: A small, lightweight daypack is handy for carrying essentials like water, sunscreen, and your camera as you explore the city's sights.

7. Spanish Phrasebook: While many locals in tourist areas speak English, having a basic Spanish phrasebook can enhance your interactions and show appreciation for the local culture.

8. Electrical Adapters: If you're traveling from a region with a different electrical outlet, pack the necessary adapters to keep your devices charged.

9. Portable Water Bottle: Staying hydrated is crucial in Cartagena's warm climate. A reusable water bottle is not only eco-friendly but also ensures you have access to water wherever you go.

10. Rain Gear: If you're visiting during the wet season, having a compact rain jacket or poncho can come in handy for sudden downpours.

11. Power Bank: Ensure your devices stay charged on the go by packing a portable power bank, especially if you plan on using your smartphone for navigation and photography.

By packing thoughtfully and considering the tropical climate, you'll be well-equipped to make the most of your Cartagena adventure, ensuring a comfortable and enjoyable experience in this enchanting city.

Entry and Visa Requirements

Before you embark on your journey to Cartagena, it's essential to be aware of the entry and visa requirements to ensure a smooth and hassle-free arrival in this vibrant city.

Entry Requirements:
As of the last update, travelers to Cartagena, Colombia, typically require a valid passport with at least six months of validity beyond their planned departure date. Ensure that your passport is in good condition and has sufficient blank pages for stamps.

Visa Requirements:
For many nationalities, Colombia allows visa-free entry for tourism purposes for a specified period. This period can vary, so it's crucial to check the specific visa regulations based on your nationality. Generally, citizens of many countries, including the United States, Canada, and most European nations, can enter Colombia for up to 90 days without a visa.

Extension of Stay:
If you wish to extend your stay beyond the initial visa-free period, it's advisable to contact the local immigration authorities in Cartagena or the nearest Colombian consulate to inquire about extension options and requirements.

Proof of Onward Travel:
While not always enforced, it's wise to have proof of onward travel, such as a return flight ticket, to demonstrate your intention to leave Colombia within the permitted timeframe.

Yellow Fever Vaccination:

Colombia may require proof of yellow fever vaccination for travelers arriving from certain countries. Ensure you check if this requirement applies to your situation and have the necessary documentation if needed.

Keep in mind that immigration policies can change, so it's essential to verify the latest regulations before your departure to Cartagena.

Currency and Language

Understanding the local currency and language in Cartagena is key to navigating the city with ease and immersing yourself in the vibrant culture.

Currency:
The official currency of Colombia is the Colombian Peso (COP). When arriving in Cartagena, it's advisable to exchange some currency at the airport or a local bank to have cash on hand. While credit cards are widely accepted in tourist areas and upscale establishments, having some cash is convenient for smaller purchases, local markets, and transportation.

Language:
The official language in Cartagena, as in the rest of Colombia, is Spanish. While many people in tourist areas and service industries may speak some English, especially in hotels and restaurants, having a few basic Spanish phrases can enhance your interactions and make your experience more enjoyable. Locals appreciate any effort to communicate in their native language, adding a personal touch to your journey.

ATMs and Currency Exchange:
ATMs are readily available in Cartagena, particularly in tourist areas and the city center. It's advisable to use ATMs affiliated with recognized banks to ensure security. Currency exchange services are also available at the airport, banks, and exchange offices in tourist areas. Be mindful of exchange rates and potential fees when exchanging money.

Tipping Culture:

Tipping is customary in Cartagena. In restaurants, a service charge may be included in the bill, but it's common to leave an additional 5-10% for good service. Tipping is also appreciated by taxi drivers, hotel staff, and tour guides.

Language Tips:
Learning a few basic Spanish phrases can go a long way in Cartagena. Simple greetings like "Hola" (Hello) and "Gracias" (Thank you) are always appreciated. If you're unsure about something, don't hesitate to ask, saying "¿Puede ayudarme?" (Can you help me?) can come in handy.

By familiarizing yourself with the local currency and embracing the Spanish language, you'll not only navigate Cartagena more smoothly but also enhance your overall experience, creating meaningful connections with the friendly locals and immersing yourself in the vibrant culture of this captivating city.

Suggested Budget

Crafting a suitable budget for your Cartagena adventure involves considering various factors to ensure you can make the most of your time in this vibrant city. Accommodation costs can vary based on your choice of neighborhood and preferences. Budget-friendly hostels in areas like Getsemani provide affordable options, while luxury hotels in the Old Town or Bocagrande may come with a higher price tag. On average, you can allocate around $30 to $150 per night, depending on your accommodation choice.

Dining in Cartagena offers a delightful culinary journey, and costs can vary based on where and what you choose to eat. Street food and local markets provide budget-friendly options, allowing you to savor authentic Colombian flavors without breaking the bank. Mid-range restaurants in tourist areas offer a diverse culinary experience, and higher-end establishments provide a more sophisticated dining atmosphere. On average, you can plan to spend between $5 to $30 per meal, depending on your dining preferences.

Transportation costs in Cartagena are generally reasonable. Local buses are an affordable option for getting around the city, with fares typically ranging from $0.70 to $1. Taxis are also relatively inexpensive, with short rides within the city costing around $3 to $7. If you plan on exploring nearby attractions or islands, boat taxis and excursions may add an extra cost to your budget. For a daily transportation budget, allocating around $10 to $20 should cover your needs.

Activities and entertainment costs will depend on your interests. Entrance fees to attractions like Castillo San Felipe de Barajas or museums may range from $5 to $15. Boat tours to the Rosario Islands or other excursions can vary in price, typically starting from $30 and going upwards. Setting aside around $20 to $50 per day for activities ensures you can explore the city's attractions and engage in various experiences.

Taking these factors into account, a daily budget of approximately $50 to $150 per person should cover accommodation, meals, transportation, and activities. Keep in mind that this is a general estimate, and your actual expenses may vary based on your personal preferences and travel style. Planning a budget that aligns with your priorities allows you to fully enjoy the enchanting allure of Cartagena without any financial worries.

Money-Saving Tips

Navigating Cartagena on a budget doesn't mean compromising on the richness of your experience. With some savvy planning, you can make the most of your journey while keeping costs in check.

1. Local Eateries and Street Food: Venture away from touristy areas to discover local eateries and street food stalls. These hidden gems not only offer authentic Colombian flavors but are also budget-friendly, allowing you to savor culinary delights without breaking the bank.

2. Free Walking Tours: Many cities, including Cartagena, offer free walking tours that provide insights into the history and culture of the area. Joining these tours is not only educational but also a cost-effective way to explore the city.

3. Explore on Foot: Cartagena's Old Town is a pedestrian's paradise, and many attractions are within walking distance. Strolling through the charming streets allows you to soak in the atmosphere without spending on transportation.

4. Local Markets: Visit local markets like Bazurto Market to experience the vibrant culture of Cartagena and find affordable souvenirs. Bargaining is common in markets, so don't hesitate to negotiate prices.

5. Public Transportation: Opt for local buses instead of taxis for short distances. Buses are a budget-friendly mode of transportation, providing a glimpse into daily life in Cartagena.

6. BYO Water Bottle: Colombia's tap water may not be suitable for drinking, but carrying a reusable water bottle and refilling it at designated water stations can save you money on buying bottled water.

7. Happy Hour: Take advantage of happy hour specials at bars and restaurants, especially those with scenic views. It's an excellent way to enjoy a drink and the ambiance without the premium price.

8. Budget Accommodations: Consider staying in budget-friendly accommodations such as hostels or guesthouses, particularly in neighborhoods like Getsemani. This not only saves money but also offers a more authentic local experience.

9. DIY City Exploration: Instead of booking expensive guided tours, explore the city on your own. Many attractions, like the Walled City, can be explored independently, allowing you to create your own itinerary.

10. Local SIM Card: If you need mobile data, consider purchasing a local SIM card for your phone. This can be more cost-effective than relying on international roaming and allows you to stay connected throughout your journey.

By incorporating these money-saving tips into your Cartagena adventure, you can enjoy the city's treasures while keeping your budget intact. It's about finding the perfect balance between exploration and financial mindfulness to make your journey both enriching and affordable.

Best Places to Book Your Trip

When it comes to booking your trip to Cartagena, choosing the right platforms can enhance your planning experience and ensure a seamless journey. Here are some of the best places to consider for booking your Cartagena adventure:

1. Skyscanner or Kayak (Flights): Start your journey by searching for the best flight deals. Skyscanner and Kayak are reliable platforms that compare prices from various airlines, helping you find the most cost-effective options for your travel dates.

2. Booking.com or Airbnb (Accommodation): Whether you prefer hotels or a more immersive local experience with Airbnb, Booking.com and Airbnb offer a wide range of accommodation options in Cartagena. From budget-friendly hostels to luxurious boutique hotels, you'll find choices that suit your preferences.

3. Expedia or Viator (Activities): Once your flights and accommodation are sorted, consider platforms like Expedia or Viator for booking activities and tours in Cartagena. These platforms provide a variety of options, from historical city tours to island-hopping adventures, allowing you to tailor your experience.

4. RentalCars or Uber (Transportation): For local transportation needs, platforms like RentalCars offer convenient options for renting a car, especially if you plan to explore beyond the city. Alternatively, Uber is available in Cartagena and can be a cost-effective and reliable choice for getting around.

5. TripAdvisor (Reviews and Recommendations): Use TripAdvisor to read reviews and get recommendations for

restaurants, attractions, and accommodations in Cartagena. The insights from fellow travelers can help you make informed decisions and uncover hidden gems.

6. Currency Exchange Platforms (Currency): Before arriving in Cartagena, consider using online currency exchange platforms to secure competitive rates. This ensures you have local currency on hand for small expenses and areas where cash is preferred.

7. Local Tour Operators (Customized Experiences): For a more personalized experience, consider reaching out to local tour operators directly. Many offer customized tours and experiences tailored to your interests, providing a unique perspective on Cartagena.

8. Travel Insurance Providers: Don't forget to invest in travel insurance to protect your trip. Platforms like World Nomads or Allianz Travel Insurance offer comprehensive coverage, including medical expenses, trip cancellations, and lost baggage.

9. Official Airline Websites: After finding the best flight deals on search engines, consider booking directly through the airline's official website. Sometimes, airlines offer exclusive promotions and perks when booking directly.

10. Local Apps (Transportation and Services): Download local apps for transportation, such as Cabify or local taxi apps, to make getting around the city more convenient. Additionally, apps like Rappi can be useful for food delivery or essential services.

By utilizing these platforms, you can efficiently plan and book every aspect of your Cartagena adventure, ensuring a well-organized and enjoyable experience in this enchanting city.

CHAPTER 2: MUST-SEE ATTRACTIONS AND LANDMARKS

Embarking on a journey through Cartagena's must-see attractions and landmarks is like stepping into a living history book where each site tells a tale of the city's rich past and vibrant present. Begin your exploration in the heart of Cartagena, the Old Town, a UNESCO World Heritage site adorned with cobblestone streets, colorful facades, and lively plazas. This enchanting area invites you to meander through its historic alleys, revealing architectural treasures that reflect the city's colonial legacy.

As you delve deeper into Cartagena's historical narrative, Castillo San Felipe de Barajas stands as a formidable sentinel overlooking the city. This iconic fortress, strategically positioned atop a hill, provides panoramic views of Cartagena and narrates stories of battles fought and won. The imposing walls that once shielded the city from pirate invasions now stand as a testament to Cartagena's resilience and strategic importance in the region.

Venturing beyond the city limits, the Rosario Islands beckon with their pristine beaches and crystal-clear waters. A boat trip to these idyllic islands offers a perfect escape, allowing you to bask in the Caribbean sun and indulge in the natural beauty that surrounds Cartagena.

Returning to the heart of the city, the historic walls that encircle Cartagena create a protective embrace around the Old Town. These walls not only offer stunning views of the city and the sea but also serve as a reminder of Cartagena's intricate defense system during its colonial era.

Continue your journey through time with visits to landmarks such as the Palacio de la Inquisición, where the city's darker historical chapters unfold, and the Convento de la Popa, perched on the city's highest hill, providing a serene retreat with panoramic views.

Stroll through Plaza Santo Domingo, where the vibrant energy of the city converges. The plaza's lively atmosphere, surrounded by restaurants and cafes, makes it an ideal spot to savor local cuisine and witness the rhythmic pulse of Cartagena's daily life.

Explore the spiritual heritage at the San Pedro Claver Church, named after the patron saint of slaves, and feel the tranquility within its historical walls. Bocagrande Beach, with its modern skyline, offers a contrast to the historic Old Town, providing a leisurely escape to sandy shores.

Wander through the colorful streets of the Getsemaní neighborhood, known for its bohemian vibe and vibrant street art. Nearby, La Boquilla Beach welcomes you with its serene coastline, inviting relaxation and water adventures.

Complete your exploration with a visit to the iconic Clock Tower (Torre del Reloj), a symbol of Cartagena's entrance, where the past seamlessly blends with the present. As you traverse these must-see attractions, each corner of Cartagena unfolds a new chapter, promising a journey filled with history, culture, and the timeless allure of the Caribbean coast.

Cartagena's Old Town

Cartagena's Old Town, a UNESCO World Heritage site, is a mesmerizing labyrinth of cobblestone streets and vibrant plazas, beckoning travelers to immerse themselves in its rich history and colonial charm. Located in the heart of the city, this historic district is a living testament to Cartagena's past and a celebration of its cultural heritage.

Navigating your way to Cartagena's Old Town is a breeze. Situated on the Caribbean coast of Colombia, the Old Town is easily accessible from various parts of the city. If you're arriving by plane, the Rafael Núñez International Airport is just a short drive away. Taxis and shuttle services are readily available, providing a convenient and efficient means of transportation to this captivating quarter.

Once you step into the Old Town, you'll find yourself surrounded by architectural wonders from the colonial era. The vibrant facades of buildings, adorned with bougainvillea, transport you to a bygone era. Wander through the enchanting alleys, discovering hidden gems like Plaza Santo Domingo, a lively square surrounded by restaurants and cafes, offering a perfect spot to soak in the local atmosphere.

As you explore, you'll encounter iconic landmarks such as the Palacio de la Inquisición, a museum showcasing the city's historical artifacts and stories. The Convento de la Popa, situated on the city's highest hill, provides not only a tranquil retreat but also panoramic views of Cartagena. The San Pedro Claver Church, dedicated to the patron saint of slaves, stands as a testament to the city's spiritual heritage.

Cartagena's Old Town isn't just about history; it's a living, breathing part of the city. The streets are adorned with street performers, musicians, and artisans, creating an immersive experience. Indulge in local cuisine at one of the many charming restaurants, offering a taste of Colombian flavors. The dynamic energy of this district, combined with its architectural allure, makes it a must-visit destination for those seeking to unravel the layers of Cartagena's captivating past.

Castillo San Felipe de Barajas

Castillo San Felipe de Barajas, a monumental fortress perched atop a hill in Cartagena, stands as an iconic symbol of the city's historical resilience and strategic significance. This impressive structure, named after King Philip IV of Spain, played a pivotal role in defending Cartagena against invasions during the colonial era.

Getting to Castillo San Felipe de Barajas is a journey that promises both historical immersion and panoramic views. Located just east of Cartagena's Old Town, the fortress is easily accessible by taxi or a leisurely walk. As you ascend the hill, the imposing walls of the castle come into view, offering a glimpse of the strategic vantage point that has safeguarded Cartagena for centuries.

Built in the 17th century, Castillo San Felipe de Barajas boasts remarkable military engineering and architectural prowess. The fortress was designed to withstand sieges and attacks, featuring a complex system of tunnels, hidden passages, and strategic vantage points. The intricacy of its design is a testament to the determination of the Spanish colonizers to protect their Caribbean stronghold.

Exploring Castillo San Felipe de Barajas is a captivating journey through history. As you wander through the labyrinthine tunnels and ascend to the various levels, you'll discover strategic viewpoints that once served as lookout posts for the defenders. The expansive views of Cartagena and the surrounding landscape from the fortress's heights provide a breathtaking panorama, making it an ideal spot for both history enthusiasts and those seeking a scenic adventure.

This formidable fortress, often regarded as the most significant military structure in the Americas, encapsulates the historical narrative of Cartagena. From its construction to the battles it witnessed, Castillo San Felipe de Barajas is a living testament to the city's ability to withstand the challenges of its past. Visiting this iconic landmark allows you to not only delve into the military history of Cartagena but also appreciate the architectural brilliance that has stood the test of time.

Rosario Islands

The Rosario Islands, an archipelago located off the coast of Cartagena, are a tropical paradise offering a serene escape from the bustling city life. Comprising 27 coral islands, the Rosario Islands boast pristine white-sand beaches, crystal-clear turquoise waters, and vibrant coral reefs, creating an idyllic setting for relaxation and exploration.

Reaching the Rosario Islands is a delightful adventure in itself. Numerous boat tours and excursions depart from Cartagena, taking you on a scenic journey over the Caribbean Sea to this tropical haven. The boat ride offers panoramic views of the coastline and a refreshing sea breeze, setting the stage for a day of sun-soaked bliss.

Upon arrival at the Rosario Islands, you'll discover a tranquil oasis surrounded by coral formations that teem with marine life. Snorkeling enthusiasts can dive into the warm waters to explore the vibrant underwater world, encountering colorful coral reefs and a variety of tropical fish. The archipelago's protected marine park status ensures the preservation of its biodiversity, providing a captivating experience for nature lovers.

Each island within the Rosario archipelago has its own unique charm. Some offer secluded beaches for a peaceful retreat, while others feature lively beach clubs with amenities like water sports and beachfront dining. Whether you seek a quiet escape or an active day of exploration, the Rosario Islands cater to various preferences, making it an ideal destination for a day trip from Cartagena.

The Rosario Islands stand as a testament to the natural beauty that graces the Caribbean coast of Colombia. This tropical paradise invites you to unwind on pristine beaches, snorkel in azure waters, and embrace the serenity of island life. A visit to the Rosario Islands ensures a rejuvenating experience, leaving you with cherished memories of the Caribbean's captivating allure.

Cartagena's Walls

Cartagena's Walls, a testament to the city's strategic defense during its colonial past, envelop the Old Town in a protective embrace, creating an iconic skyline against the Caribbean backdrop. These historic fortifications, declared a UNESCO World Heritage site, offer not only a glimpse into the city's military history but also stunning views and a unique exploration opportunity.

Located in the heart of Cartagena, the walls are easily accessible from various points within the Old Town. Walking along the cobblestone streets, you'll encounter the fortifications at different intervals, providing a continuous link to the city's historical narrative. As you approach the walls, their sheer scale becomes evident, showcasing the architectural ingenuity employed to safeguard Cartagena from pirate invasions.

One of the most iconic sections of the walls is near the Clock Tower (Torre del Reloj), a symbol of Cartagena's entrance. This location serves as a popular starting point for those looking to embark on a leisurely stroll along the fortifications. The views from the walls are nothing short of spectacular, offering panoramic glimpses of the Old Town's rooftops, the Caribbean Sea, and the modern skyline beyond.

Walking along Cartagena's Walls is a journey through time, with opportunities to appreciate not only the city's fortifications but also its vibrant present. Locals and tourists alike frequent these walls for a leisurely stroll, adding to the lively atmosphere. Street vendors offer refreshments, creating a charming ambiance as you absorb the scenic beauty.

As you traverse the walls, you'll encounter various entry points that lead to hidden plazas, historical landmarks, and charming corners within the Old Town. It's a self-guided exploration, allowing you to set your own pace and discover the magic of Cartagena from this elevated vantage point.

Whether you're seeking a tranquil moment to take in the views, capturing stunning photographs, or simply immersing yourself in the city's ambiance, a visit to Cartagena's Walls is a quintessential experience. This historical treasure not only preserves the city's past but also provides a dynamic and scenic backdrop for those looking to appreciate the timeless allure of Cartagena.

Palacio de la Inquisición

The Palacio de la Inquisición, nestled within the heart of Cartagena's Old Town, is a striking colonial building that holds within its walls a compelling and, at times, dark chapter of the city's history. Constructed in the early 18th century, this grand edifice served as the headquarters of the Spanish Inquisition in Cartagena, overseeing investigations and trials deemed heretical by the Catholic Church.

Finding the Palacio de la Inquisición is a journey into the past, as it is conveniently located in the central Plaza de Bolívar. The address, Plaza de Bolívar, Cartagena, is a reference point for those seeking to delve into the historical nuances of the city. As you approach the plaza, the imposing façade of the palace, adorned with balconies and ornate details, commands attention, hinting at the stories concealed within.

Venturing inside the Palacio de la Inquisición reveals a museum that sheds light on the inquisitorial practices of the time. The exhibits showcase artifacts and historical documentation, providing insight into the methods employed during the Spanish Inquisition. The museum, while confronting the darker aspects of Cartagena's past, also celebrates the resilience and transformation of the city over the centuries.

While at the Palacio de la Inquisición, visitors can explore the various rooms that once hosted inquisitorial proceedings. The Sala de Torturas (Torture Room) is a chilling reminder of the methods used to extract confessions, while other chambers house exhibits on the history of Cartagena and its diverse cultural influences.

Beyond its historical significance, the Palacio de la Inquisición stands as a cultural landmark within the Old Town. The architecture itself, with its colonial charm, offers a glimpse into the grandeur of the city's past. As visitors navigate the museum's halls, they encounter a nuanced blend of architecture, history, and culture that captures the essence of Cartagena's multifaceted identity.

A visit to the Palacio de la Inquisición invites reflection on the complexities of Cartagena's history while appreciating the resilience and vibrancy that define the city today. It is an essential stop for those who seek a comprehensive understanding of Cartagena's past within the context of its present cultural richness.

Convento de la Popa

Perched atop the highest hill in Cartagena, the Convento de la Popa stands as a serene sanctuary with panoramic views that offer a breathtaking perspective of the city and its surroundings. This historic convent, founded in the early 17th century, holds a tranquil ambiance and spiritual significance, inviting visitors to connect with both Cartagena's religious heritage and its stunning natural beauty.

Finding your way to the Convento de la Popa is a journey of ascent, adding a touch of adventure to your visit. Located on Cerro de La Popa, the address is Convento de La Popa, Cerro de La Popa, Cartagena, emphasizing the elevated location that provides the convent with its commanding views. Taxis or guided tours are common choices for reaching this hilltop sanctuary, where you'll encounter a peaceful retreat away from the bustling city below.

The Convento de la Popa, with its whitewashed walls and timeless architecture, invites contemplation as you explore its courtyards, chapels, and gardens. The convent is dedicated to Our Lady of Candelaria, and the chapel houses an altar adorned with intricate gold leaf detailing, creating a visually striking and spiritually evocative space.

The true allure of the Convento de la Popa lies in its elevated terraces, which offer unrivaled panoramic views of Cartagena and the Caribbean Sea. The sweeping vistas encompass the Old Town's historic rooftops, the modern skyline, and the vast expanse of the sea, providing a stunning backdrop for reflection and photography.

Beyond its religious and historical significance, the Convento de la Popa contributes to Cartagena's cultural tapestry. Its serene atmosphere and well-maintained gardens make it an ideal place for quiet contemplation, offering a serene escape from the city's vibrant streets.

A visit to the Convento de la Popa allows you to witness the intersection of spiritual heritage and natural beauty. It is a testament to Cartagena's ability to preserve its historical treasures while providing a tranquil retreat for those seeking both cultural enrichment and moments of peace amid the scenic splendor of the Caribbean coast.

Plaza Santo Domingo

Plaza Santo Domingo, a vibrant and lively square nestled within Cartagena's Old Town, encapsulates the dynamic energy and cultural richness of the city. Surrounded by charming colonial buildings, bustling cafes, and artful sculptures, this iconic plaza is a hub of activity, inviting both locals and visitors to soak in its spirited ambiance.

Located at the heart of the Old Town, Plaza Santo Domingo is easily accessible from various points within the city. The address is Plaza Santo Domingo, Cartagena, serving as a central reference for those looking to immerse themselves in the lively atmosphere of this historic square. Whether you approach from the narrow streets of the Old Town or the bustling avenues nearby, the plaza beckons with its inviting charm.

The focal point of Plaza Santo Domingo is the prominent sculpture "La Gorda Gertrudis" created by renowned Colombian artist Fernando Botero. This voluptuous bronze figure adds a playful touch to the square, becoming a popular meeting spot and a symbol of Cartagena's embrace of art and culture.

Surrounding the plaza, an array of outdoor cafes and restaurants spill out onto the cobblestone streets, offering al fresco dining and a front-row seat to the vibrant street life. The atmosphere is infused with the sounds of live music, street performers, and the laughter of locals and tourists alike, creating a lively backdrop for socializing and people-watching.

Plaza Santo Domingo's lively character extends into the evening, with the surrounding establishments illuminated and the plaza itself becoming a hub for nighttime entertainment. Whether you're enjoying a leisurely coffee in the morning, savoring a traditional Colombian meal in the afternoon, or reveling in the spirited nightlife after sunset, Plaza Santo Domingo stands as a versatile and captivating space within the heart of Cartagena's Old Town.

A visit to Plaza Santo Domingo is not just a stop on the map; it's an immersive experience into the heart of Cartagena's cultural tapestry. It's a place where history meets contemporary vibrancy, offering a perfect snapshot of the city's unique blend of tradition, art, and social engagement.

San Pedro Claver Church

San Pedro Claver Church, a historic and spiritually significant landmark in Cartagena, pays homage to the city's colonial past and the enduring legacy of Saint Peter Claver. Named after the Spanish Jesuit priest who dedicated his life to serving enslaved Africans, this church stands as a symbol of compassion, social justice, and spiritual devotion.

Located within the Old Town, San Pedro Claver Church is easily accessible from various points within Cartagena. The address is Iglesia San Pedro Claver, Carrera 4 # 31-00, Cartagena, emphasizing its central location within the historic district. As you approach the church, its Baroque-style façade and intricate details invite contemplation, setting the stage for a visit that combines architectural beauty with historical resonance.

Stepping inside San Pedro Claver Church is a journey into both religious history and cultural heritage. The church, dating back to the 17th century, showcases a harmonious blend of architectural styles, with elements of Spanish Colonial, Moorish, and Gothic influences. The interior is adorned with religious art, golden altars, and symbolic imagery, creating a serene and spiritually evocative atmosphere.

The church also houses the remains of Saint Peter Claver in a glass coffin, paying tribute to the man who devoted his life to advocating for the rights and dignity of enslaved individuals. Visitors can explore the various chapels, admire the religious artwork, and reflect on the profound impact of Saint Peter Claver's humanitarian work.

Adjacent to the church is the San Pedro Claver Convent, which serves as a museum. This museum provides additional insights into the life and legacy of Saint Peter Claver, offering a comprehensive understanding of his contributions to Cartagena's social and religious history.

Beyond its religious significance, San Pedro Claver Church contributes to Cartagena's cultural landscape. The church hosts concerts, exhibitions, and cultural events, inviting both locals and visitors to engage with the vibrant cultural scene within the Old Town.

A visit to San Pedro Claver Church is a multifaceted experience, encompassing history, spirituality, and cultural appreciation. It offers a moment of reflection on the city's past while celebrating the enduring impact of individuals like Saint Peter Claver, whose legacy continues to resonate in the heart of Cartagena.

Bocagrande Beach

Bocagrande Beach, a vibrant stretch of golden sands along the shores of Cartagena, offers a contemporary seaside experience, blending urban sophistication with the allure of the Caribbean Sea. This bustling beachfront, characterized by modern high-rises and a lively atmosphere, provides both locals and tourists with a dynamic setting for leisure and recreation.

Located southwest of the Old Town, Bocagrande Beach is easily accessible from various parts of Cartagena. The address is Playa Bocagrande, Cartagena, emphasizing its central location along the Bocagrande peninsula. Whether you're staying in the nearby hotels, exploring the city, or seeking a beach day escape, Bocagrande Beach beckons with its inviting shoreline.

The beach is known for its wide expanse of soft sands and warm Caribbean waters, creating an ideal environment for sunbathing, swimming, and water activities. Bocagrande's urban backdrop adds a unique flair to the beach experience, with high-end hotels, restaurants, and shops lining the waterfront, providing a blend of relaxation and cosmopolitan charm.

For those seeking an active day by the sea, Bocagrande Beach offers opportunities for water sports such as jet skiing, parasailing, and paddleboarding. The beach's lively ambiance extends into the evening, with beachfront bars and restaurants offering a perfect setting to enjoy a sunset cocktail or a delightful meal with views of the Caribbean.

Bocagrande Beach's proximity to the Old Town allows visitors to seamlessly transition from exploring the historical sites to indulging in a beach retreat. The juxtaposition of historical charm and modern sophistication creates a distinctive atmosphere that sets Bocagrande apart as a unique beach destination within Cartagena.

While the beach may lack the colonial architecture found in the Old Town, its contemporary appeal and lively energy make it a popular choice for those seeking a more cosmopolitan beach experience. Whether you're looking for a relaxing day under the sun, water adventures, or a vibrant beachfront atmosphere, Bocagrande Beach offers a diverse and captivating escape along the Caribbean coast of Cartagena.

Getsemaní Neighborhood

Getsemaní, an eclectic and bohemian neighborhood nestled just outside Cartagena's Old Town, invites visitors to experience a dynamic blend of history, culture, and vibrant street life. This spirited district, known for its colorful facades, street art, and lively plazas, offers a unique perspective on Cartagena's contemporary identity.

Located southeast of the Old Town, Getsemaní is easily accessible by foot, making it a seamless extension of the historic city center. The neighborhood's streets are characterized by narrow alleys and colonial-era architecture, providing an authentic backdrop for exploration. The address is Barrio Getsemaní, Cartagena, symbolizing the neighborhood's integral role in the city's cultural tapestry.

Getsemaní's charm lies in its ability to seamlessly blend the old and the new. As you wander through its streets, you'll encounter vibrant murals and street art that adorn the facades, contributing to the neighborhood's artistic and bohemian ambiance. These visual expressions often convey social messages, reflecting the neighborhood's history and its contemporary cultural movements.

One of the central hubs of Getsemaní is Plaza de la Trinidad, a lively square surrounded by cafes, bars, and a church. This plaza serves as a gathering place for locals and visitors alike, with live music performances, street vendors, and a convivial atmosphere that encapsulates the neighborhood's vibrant spirit.

Getsemaní is not just a feast for the eyes; it's also a culinary and nightlife destination. The neighborhood boasts a diverse array of restaurants, from traditional Colombian eateries serving local delicacies to trendy establishments offering international cuisine. As the sun sets, Getsemaní comes alive with a burgeoning nightlife scene, where lively bars and clubs attract those seeking to dance and celebrate into the early hours.

Beyond its visual and culinary allure, Getsemaní holds historical significance. The neighborhood was once home to slaves and working-class residents, contributing to its diverse cultural heritage. Today, Getsemaní stands as a testament to Cartagena's ability to evolve while preserving the authenticity and vitality that define its streets.

A visit to Getsemaní is an immersion into the soul of Cartagena, where history, art, and contemporary culture converge. Whether you're exploring its streets by day, savoring local flavors in its eateries, or embracing the vibrant nightlife, Getsemaní beckons as a dynamic and essential facet of Cartagena's cultural mosaic.

La Boquilla Beach

La Boquilla Beach, a serene coastal retreat just a short distance from Cartagena, offers a tranquil escape along the shores of the Caribbean. Known for its pristine sands, clear waters, and relaxed atmosphere, this beach destination provides a peaceful respite from the bustling city life, inviting visitors to unwind and embrace the natural beauty of the Colombian coast.

Located northeast of the Old Town, La Boquilla Beach is easily accessible by taxi or a short drive from Cartagena. The address is Playa La Boquilla, Cartagena, emphasizing the idyllic setting along the La Boquilla peninsula. Whether you're seeking a day of relaxation, water activities, or a scenic getaway, La Boquilla Beach beckons with its laid-back charm.

The beach itself is characterized by soft, golden sands that stretch along the coastline, creating a perfect setting for sunbathing and beachcombing. The warm Caribbean waters invite swimmers to enjoy a refreshing dip, while the gentle waves provide a soothing soundtrack to the coastal experience.

La Boquilla Beach stands out for its serene ambiance, as it is less crowded compared to some of the more central beaches. This tranquility allows visitors to fully immerse themselves in the natural beauty that surrounds the area, making it an ideal spot for those seeking a quieter beach escape.

For those who enjoy water sports, La Boquilla Beach offers opportunities for activities such as kayaking and paddleboarding. The calm waters and scenic backdrop create an ideal environment for both beginners and enthusiasts to explore the coastline from a different perspective.

The beach is also lined with rustic seafood restaurants and beachfront huts, providing a chance to savor local flavors and indulge in fresh catches from the sea. These establishments contribute to the authentic and unspoiled character of La Boquilla Beach, offering a genuine taste of coastal life.

A visit to La Boquilla Beach is a retreat into simplicity and natural beauty. Whether you're basking in the sun, exploring the coastline, or enjoying the local cuisine, this beach destination captures the essence of a peaceful seaside escape, making it a cherished haven for those seeking a tranquil day along the shores of Cartagena.

Clock Tower (Torre del Reloj)

The Clock Tower (Torre del Reloj), a symbolic gateway to Cartagena's Old Town, stands as an iconic landmark that welcomes visitors into the heart of this historic city. This architectural marvel, dating back to the 17th century, serves not only as a timekeeper but also as a testament to the rich history and cultural heritage that awaits within the cobblestone streets of the Old Town.

Situated at the main entrance of the walled city, the Clock Tower is a pivotal point for those arriving by land. The address is Torre del Reloj, Plaza de la Aduana, Cartagena, emphasizing its location at the intersection of the bustling Plaza de la Aduana, the historical and administrative center of Cartagena.

As you approach the Clock Tower, its ornate design and distinctive arched entrance immediately capture the imagination. The tower was once part of the city's defensive fortifications, and its strategic position allowed guards to monitor those entering and leaving the city. Today, it stands as a welcoming symbol, inviting visitors to step through its arches and embark on a journey through time.

The Plaza de la Aduana, surrounding the Clock Tower, is a bustling square adorned with historic buildings, lively cafes, and local vendors. This vibrant atmosphere encapsulates the essence of Cartagena's Old Town, where the past seamlessly integrates with the present.

Passing through the Clock Tower, visitors find themselves immersed in the charming streets of the Old Town, with its colorful facades, inviting plazas, and hidden treasures waiting to be discovered. The Clock Tower marks the beginning of an enchanting exploration, where each corner reveals a story, and each cobblestone narrates the city's colonial legacy.

The Clock Tower also serves as a focal point for cultural events, gatherings, and celebrations, further solidifying its role as a dynamic and symbolic landmark within Cartagena. Whether you're capturing a photograph against its historic backdrop, enjoying a leisurely stroll through the Plaza de la Aduana, or entering the Old Town to uncover its hidden gems, the Clock Tower is an essential starting point for anyone seeking to experience the timeless charm of Cartagena.

CHAPTER 3: ACCOMMODATION OPTIONS

Immersing yourself in the captivating allure of Cartagena requires not just a visit but a stay that complements the city's vibrant spirit. Cartagena offers a spectrum of accommodation options catering to diverse preferences and budgets. For those seeking the epitome of indulgence, the city boasts an array of luxurious hotels and resorts. From opulent suites with breathtaking views of the Caribbean to lavish amenities that pamper your every need, these establishments provide a sumptuous backdrop for an unforgettable Cartagena experience.

If you're mindful of your travel budget, fear not—Cartagena warmly welcomes budget-conscious travelers with open arms. The city is dotted with charming hostels, cozy guesthouses, and budget-friendly hotels that offer comfort without breaking the bank. These accommodations not only provide a restful haven after a day of exploration but also facilitate a more immersive connection with the local culture, as you interact with fellow travelers and share stories of your Cartagena escapades.

For those yearning for a more authentic and unique experience, Cartagena unveils a treasure trove of distinctive stays and local favorites. From boutique hotels infused with colonial charm to cozy bed and breakfasts nestled in the heart of neighborhoods like Getsemaní, these accommodations immerse you in the city's local flavor. Your stay becomes more than just a night's rest; it transforms into a cultural journey, allowing you to absorb the colors, sounds, and stories that define Cartagena's rich tapestry.

Choosing the perfect accommodation is not just about a bed for the night; it's about curating an experience that aligns with your travel aspirations. Consider factors like location, amenities, and the unique character of each option. Whether you're drawn to the lavish comforts of luxury, the frugality of budget-friendly choices, or the charm of local favorites, Cartagena's accommodations beckon with open arms, ready to weave their own chapter into the story of your unforgettable journey.

So, as you embark on this adventure, let your choice of accommodation become a cornerstone of your Cartagena escapade, enriching your travel narrative with comfort, character, and the warm embrace of Colombian hospitality.

Best Luxury Hotels and Resorts

Indulgence in Cartagena reaches new heights through its array of luxurious hotels and resorts, promising a stay that mirrors the opulence of the city's history and culture. As you explore the options available for those seeking the pinnacle of accommodation, a world of sumptuous experiences awaits, each venue offering its unique blend of comfort and sophistication.

Charleston Santa Teresa Hotel Cartagena: This five-star gem, located at Carrera 3 No. 31-23, within the historic Old Town, stands as an architectural masterpiece. With its colonial-style architecture and plush interiors, it seamlessly marries historic charm with modern elegance. Getting there is a breeze, and once you step inside, you're greeted with exquisite courtyards, a rooftop pool with panoramic views, and luxurious spa facilities. Immerse yourself in Cartagena's history with a stay at this refined establishment.

Hotel Sofitel Legend Santa Clara: Nestled at Calle Del Torno No. 39-29, this former convent turned five-star hotel is a testament to timeless luxury. Surrounded by the city's historic walls, it effortlessly blends historic charm with contemporary comfort. The hotel's spa, multiple dining options, and the picturesque pool beckon for relaxation. From here, exploring Cartagena's Old Town becomes a seamless journey through its cobblestone streets and vibrant plazas.

Casa San Agustin: Tucked away at Calle de la Universidad No. 36-44, this boutique hotel captures the essence of Cartagena's colonial past. With only 30 rooms, it ensures an intimate and exclusive experience. The hotel boasts a rooftop pool, elegant courtyards, and rooms adorned with handcrafted furnishings.

Your stay here offers not just accommodation but an immersive journey into Cartagena's cultural and architectural heritage.

Hyatt Regency Cartagena: Positioned at Carrera 1 #12-118, this modern luxury hotel graces the Bocagrande district, offering a contemporary retreat by the Caribbean Sea. The sleek design and ocean-view rooms set the stage for a stylish stay. The infinity pool overlooking the sea, the spa, and the hotel's beach club elevate the experience. Here, the vibrancy of Bocagrande meets the comfort of upscale living.

Ananda Hotel Boutique: Situated at Calle del Cuartel No. 36-77, this boutique gem combines colonial aesthetics with modern sophistication. With only seven rooms, it ensures an exclusive stay. The rooftop terrace, complete with a pool and lounge area, provides a serene escape. Delight in personalized service and a tranquil ambiance that defines this boutique haven in the heart of Cartagena.

These luxury accommodations not only offer lavish interiors and top-notch amenities but also serve as gateways to Cartagena's most enchanting attractions. Your stay becomes a seamless blend of historical exploration, culinary indulgence, and the embrace of coastal beauty, ensuring that every moment in Cartagena is nothing short of extraordinary.

Budget-Friendly Accommodations

For those seeking a delightful stay in Cartagena without breaking the bank, the city opens its arms to a variety of budget-friendly accommodations. From cozy hostels to affordable hotels, these options ensure that your journey is not just economical but also filled with comfort and charm.

El Viajero Hostel Cartagena: Located at Getsemaní, Calle 29 #10b-39, this vibrant hostel offers budget-conscious travelers a lively atmosphere and a central location. Getsemaní's spirited neighborhood sets the backdrop for your stay, and from here, the Old Town is just a stroll away. Dormitory-style rooms and communal spaces encourage interaction among fellow travelers, fostering a sense of camaraderie that defines the hostel experience.

Hotel San Roque: Nestled at Calle del Estanco del Aguardiente #35-33, this budget-friendly hotel in the heart of the Old Town provides simplicity without sacrificing convenience. The hotel's traditional architecture and comfortable rooms offer a welcoming retreat after a day of exploration. With its central location, you can effortlessly explore Cartagena's historic sites, plazas, and vibrant streets.

Hostal Casa Baluarte: Situated at Calle Baluarte Santo Domingo #33-28, this charming guesthouse is a testament to affordability without compromising on character. The colonial-style building exudes a cozy ambiance, and its location in the heart of the Old Town ensures easy access to Cartagena's iconic attractions. Immerse yourself in the city's history without straining your budget.

Casa Viena: Found at Calle Cochera del Hobo #38-66, this budget-friendly guesthouse in Getsemaní offers a quaint escape with a personalized touch. The simplicity of Casa Viena is complemented by its warm hospitality, creating a home-like environment for guests. Getsemaní's lively surroundings and proximity to local eateries add an authentic flavor to your stay.

El Genoves Hostal: Positioned at Calle Cochera del Hobo #38-23, this hostel in Getsemaní strikes a balance between affordability and a vibrant social atmosphere. The hostel's communal spaces, including a rooftop terrace, provide a relaxed setting for interaction and relaxation. Dive into Getsemaní's artistic spirit and immerse yourself in the local culture from this well-situated budget-friendly option.

These budget-friendly accommodations not only offer practicality but also serve as gateways to the heart of Cartagena. Embrace the city's charm without straining your wallet, ensuring that your stay becomes an enriching experience where affordability meets the warmth of Colombian hospitality.

Unique Stays and Local Favorites

Cartagena, with its rich tapestry of culture and history, offers an array of unique stays and local favorites that promise a distinctive and immersive experience. From boutique gems to hidden treasures, these accommodations provide an authentic glimpse into the soul of the city, elevating your stay to a cultural journey filled with charm and character.

Casa Canabal Hotel Boutique: Tucked away at Calle Del Sargento Mayor No. 6-87, this boutique hotel in the heart of the Old Town exudes elegance and local charm. The meticulously restored colonial building boasts stylish interiors, creating a luxurious yet authentic atmosphere. Embrace the essence of Cartagena as you wander through nearby plazas, enjoy the hotel's courtyard oasis, and savor the local flavors offered by its restaurant.

Hotel Quadrifolio: Positioned at Calle del Cuartel No. 36-118, this intimate boutique hotel offers a luxurious retreat within the Old Town's historical confines. With just eight suites, each uniquely decorated, Hotel Quadrifolio provides a personalized experience. Its central location ensures that Cartagena's landmarks are within easy reach, while the hotel itself becomes a sanctuary of comfort and sophistication.

Casa Lola Deluxe Gallery: Found at Calle del Torno No. 39-29, this boutique hotel seamlessly combines contemporary art with historical ambiance. Each room serves as a canvas, adorned with unique artwork by Colombian artists. The hotel's location within the Old Town allows for easy exploration of nearby attractions, and its rooftop terrace provides panoramic views of the city's rooftops and domes.

Selina Cartagena: Located at Calle Larga No. 8A-141, Selina Cartagena is not just a place to stay but a vibrant cultural hub. This unique accommodation concept offers a blend of co-living, co-working, and cultural immersion. With its eclectic design, art-filled spaces, and a calendar of events, Selina becomes a focal point for creatives and travelers seeking a dynamic and social experience in the heart of Cartagena.

Hotel Casa San Agustin: Situated at Calle de la Universidad No. 36-44, this boutique hotel is a harmonious blend of colonial history and contemporary luxury. With only 30 rooms, it ensures an exclusive experience within the heart of the Old Town. The hotel's meticulous preservation of historical architecture and artistic details creates a timeless ambiance that reflects the soul of Cartagena.

These unique stays and local favorites not only offer a place to rest but also serve as gateways to Cartagena's essence. Immerse yourself in the city's cultural vibrancy, explore its hidden corners, and let the character of these accommodations weave a narrative that resonates with the authentic spirit of Cartagena.

Tips for Choosing the Perfect Accommodation

Choosing the perfect accommodation in Cartagena is more than just selecting a place to stay; it's about curating an experience that aligns with your travel aspirations. Consider these tips to ensure your choice complements the enchanting journey that awaits in this vibrant Colombian city.

Location Matters: Cartagena is a city with diverse neighborhoods, each offering a unique atmosphere. If you're drawn to the historic charm of cobblestone streets and colonial architecture, consider accommodations within the Old Town. For a more modern and beachside vibe, areas like Bocagrande may be your preference. Getsemaní, with its artistic flair and local energy, provides a bohemian experience. Choose a location that aligns with your interests and allows easy access to the attractions you plan to explore.

Budget Wisely: Determine your budget early on and look for accommodations that not only fit within your financial plan but also offer good value for money. Cartagena caters to a range of budgets, from luxury hotels to budget-friendly hostels. Remember that spending a bit more for a central location or unique amenities can enhance your overall experience.

Read Reviews: Take advantage of online platforms and read reviews from fellow travelers. Their insights can provide valuable information about the accommodation's cleanliness, customer service, and overall experience. Look for consistent positive feedback and consider any potential concerns raised by previous guests.

Amenities that Matter: Consider the amenities that are important to you. Whether it's a rooftop pool, a central courtyard, or proximity to the beach, prioritize the features that will enhance your stay. Check if the accommodation offers services such as airport transfers, guided tours, or on-site dining that align with your preferences.

Local Character: If you seek an immersive experience, consider accommodations that reflect the local culture and history. Boutique hotels within colonial buildings, guesthouses in vibrant neighborhoods, or eco-friendly stays can add an extra layer of authenticity to your Cartagena adventure.

Flexibility in Booking: Given the uncertainties of travel, especially in Cartagena's peak seasons, opt for accommodations with flexible booking policies. This allows you to adapt your plans without unnecessary stress if unexpected changes arise.

Connectivity: In today's digital age, connectivity is crucial. Check if the accommodation provides reliable Wi-Fi, especially if you plan on working remotely or sharing your travel experiences online. A stable internet connection can enhance your overall convenience during your stay.

By considering these tips, you can navigate the myriad of accommodation options in Cartagena with confidence, ensuring that your chosen stay becomes an integral part of your unforgettable journey in this captivating Colombian city.

CHAPTER 4: DINING AND CUISINE

Embark on a culinary journey through Cartagena, where dining is not just a necessity but a celebration of the city's rich cultural tapestry. From tucked-away eateries to high-end restaurants, Cartagena's dining scene caters to every palate, promising a fusion of flavors that mirrors the city's vibrant spirit. Explore the best restaurants and eateries, each offering a unique gastronomic experience that showcases the diversity of Colombian cuisine.

Cartagena's culinary landscape is a treasure trove of local delicacies waiting to be savored. Dive into the must-try flavors of the city, from the iconic Arepa de Huevo, a savory deep-fried cornmeal pocket filled with egg and meat, to the refreshing Ceviche Cartagenero, a seafood delight marinated in lime juice and coconut milk. Local markets and street corners unveil a world of culinary delights, providing an authentic taste of Cartagena's gastronomic heritage.

As you indulge in Cartagena's culinary offerings, consider elevating your dining experience by seeking establishments with mesmerizing views. Whether it's a seaside dinner along Bocagrande's promenade or a rooftop terrace overlooking the historic Old Town, dining with a view adds an extra layer of enchantment to your meal. Immerse yourself in the city's beauty as you savor local delicacies against a backdrop of Caribbean sunsets or colonial architecture.

In Cartagena, dining etiquette is an art, and local foodie tips can enhance your culinary exploration. Embrace the unhurried pace of meals, allowing time for conversation and savoring each bite. Engage with locals to discover hidden gems, as they often hold the keys to the best-kept culinary secrets. Don't shy away from street food; instead, let the aroma of fresh empanadas or grilled arepas guide your culinary adventures. In Cartagena, dining is not just about sustenance; it's a sensory celebration that invites you to savor the flavors, appreciate the views, and embrace the local warmth that defines Colombian hospitality.

Best Restaurants and Eateries

Embark on a culinary odyssey through Cartagena's best restaurants and eateries, where every bite tells a story and flavors dance on your palate. The city's diverse dining scene invites you to savor both traditional Colombian dishes and innovative culinary creations, ensuring an unforgettable gastronomic experience.

La Vitrola: Nestled in the heart of the Old Town at Calle Baloco No. 33-201, La Vitrola is a culinary institution that transports you to a bygone era. This iconic restaurant exudes timeless elegance, featuring live Cuban music and an extensive menu showcasing Caribbean and Colombian cuisine. With its classic charm, La Vitrola offers not just a meal but a cultural immersion within the historic walls of Cartagena.

Carmen: Located at Calle del Santisimo No. 8-19, Carmen is a culinary gem where innovation meets tradition. This Michelin-starred restaurant, housed in a colonial mansion, boasts a sophisticated ambiance. The menu, curated by Chef Carmen Angel, harmonizes local ingredients with global influences. Indulge in the tasting menu for a culinary journey that reflects the city's rich cultural heritage.

El Boliche Cebicheria: Situated at Carrera 7 No. 32-16, this vibrant eatery in the heart of Getsemaní celebrates the coastal flavors of Cartagena. El Boliche Cebicheria specializes in ceviche, showcasing the freshest seafood with a Colombian twist. The colorful decor and lively atmosphere create a perfect setting for enjoying this seaside delicacy and immersing yourself in the local culinary scene.

Alma: Perched at Calle del Porvenir No. 35-37, Alma offers a contemporary dining experience within the Old Town. The restaurant's stylish interiors and eclectic menu showcase a fusion of international and Caribbean flavors. From inventive cocktails to beautifully presented dishes, Alma invites diners to explore the modern side of Cartagena's culinary evolution.

Don Juan: Found at Calle del Colegio No. 34-60, Don Juan is a culinary haven that pays homage to traditional Colombian cuisine. This family-run restaurant, housed in a colonial mansion, invites you to savor time-honored recipes passed down through generations. The cozy atmosphere and the extensive menu of Colombian classics make Don Juan a beloved stop for those seeking an authentic taste of the country.

These establishments not only offer exceptional cuisine but also provide a glimpse into the diverse influences that shape Cartagena's culinary identity. From historic venues in the Old Town to trendy eateries in vibrant neighborhoods, each restaurant and eatery contributes to the city's reputation as a gastronomic destination worth savoring.

Must-Try Local Delicacies

Delve into the vibrant tapestry of Cartagena's culinary heritage by indulging in a selection of must-try local delicacies that captivate the essence of Colombian flavors. From street-side stalls to quaint eateries, these dishes offer a symphony of tastes that will leave a lasting impression on your palate.

Arepa de Huevo: A quintessential street food delight, the Arepa de Huevo is a savory fried cornmeal pocket filled with egg and minced meat. Locals often enjoy this handheld treat as a quick and flavorful snack. Visit street vendors or local markets to experience the authentic preparation of this beloved Colombian dish.

Ceviche Cartagenero: Seafood enthusiasts rejoice in the flavors of Ceviche Cartagenero, a refreshing dish that embodies the coastal essence of the city. Marinated in lime juice and coconut milk, the ceviche features a medley of fresh fish, shrimp, and octopus. Savor this culinary delight at seaside restaurants or seafood stalls for an authentic taste of Cartagena's coastal cuisine.

Bandeja Paisa: While originally from the Antioquia region, Bandeja Paisa is a hearty dish that has found its way into Cartagena's culinary scene. This robust platter typically includes rice, beans, ground meat, chorizo, fried egg, plantains, and avocado. Satisfy your appetite for traditional Colombian fare by seeking out local restaurants that serve this flavorful and filling dish.

Ajiaco: A comforting soup that reflects the country's diverse culinary influences, Ajiaco is a must-try for those seeking a taste of Colombia's traditional flavors. This hearty soup typically features chicken, three types of potatoes, corn on the cob, and herbs. Look for local eateries that specialize in traditional Colombian cuisine to experience the warmth and richness of Ajiaco.

Buñuelos: Conclude your culinary exploration with the sweet delight of Buñuelos, delightful fried dough balls that are crispy on the outside and soft on the inside. Often enjoyed as a snack or dessert, these golden treats are dusted with sugar and offer a perfect balance of sweetness. Seek out local bakeries or street vendors to experience the irresistible allure of Buñuelos.

These local delicacies encapsulate the diverse and vibrant culinary landscape of Cartagena. Whether you're strolling through bustling markets, enjoying a meal at a traditional eatery, or sampling street food delights, these dishes invite you to savor the unique flavors that define the gastronomic identity of this enchanting Colombian city.

Dining with a View

Elevate your dining experience in Cartagena by seeking out establishments that offer not just delectable cuisine but also stunning views, creating a sensory feast for both your taste buds and your eyes. Whether it's the historic Old Town, the Caribbean Sea, or charming rooftops, dining with a view in Cartagena adds an extra layer of enchantment to your culinary journey.

Cafe del Mar: Perched on the historic walls of Cartagena with an address at Baluarte de Santo Domingo, Cafe del Mar is an iconic venue renowned for its breathtaking sunset views over the Caribbean Sea. Enjoy a refreshing cocktail as you watch the sun dip below the horizon, casting hues of orange and pink over the water. This open-air cafe provides an unforgettable panorama, making it a favorite spot for those seeking a romantic and picturesque dining experience.

Movich Hotel Rooftop Bar: Located at Centro, Calle Velez Danies #33-66, the Movich Hotel Rooftop Bar offers a sophisticated setting with panoramic views of the Old Town. As you savor international and Colombian dishes, including fresh seafood and grilled specialties, you'll be treated to a captivating backdrop of colonial architecture and the vibrant streets below. The rooftop ambiance provides a perfect blend of elegance and relaxation.

Alquimico: Situated at Calle del Colegio #34-24, Alquimico is not just a bar; it's an experiential journey set against the charming backdrop of Getsemaní. Ascend to the rooftop terrace, where lush greenery and a trendy atmosphere create an intimate setting. The view encompasses the colorful facades of Getsemaní and offers a unique perspective of Cartagena's urban charm. Pair your evening with creative cocktails and tapas, creating a memorable blend of flavors and aesthetics.

Candelaria Gastrobar: Found at Centro, Calle Estanco del Aguardiente #35-30, Candelaria Gastrobar combines gourmet dining with panoramic views of Cartagena's historic rooftops. This cozy and stylish venue is nestled within the Old Town, providing an intimate setting for enjoying Colombian and international cuisine. Sip on carefully crafted cocktails and relish the city's timeless charm as you dine amidst the colonial architecture.

Epoca Espresso Bar: If you prefer a view that embraces the lively streets of Getsemaní, visit Epoca Espresso Bar at Calle Larga #8B-45. This charming coffee shop with a rooftop terrace offers not only exceptional Colombian coffee but also a front-row seat to the vibrant energy of Getsemaní's streets. Enjoy a leisurely brunch or a cup of coffee while immersing yourself in the neighborhood's artistic and bohemian atmosphere.

These dining venues not only showcase the culinary prowess of Cartagena but also provide an opportunity to relish the city's beauty from unique vantage points. Whether you're celebrating a special occasion or simply enjoying a leisurely meal, dining with a view in Cartagena is an experience that engages all your senses.

Dining Etiquette and Local Foodie Tips

Embrace the cultural nuances of Cartagena's dining scene by navigating the local etiquette and savoring insider tips that will enhance your culinary journey in this vibrant Colombian city.

Unhurried Pace: When dining in Cartagena, embrace the unhurried pace of meals. Locals cherish their time spent dining, often engaging in lengthy conversations over the table. Allow yourself the luxury of enjoying each bite and savoring the flavors without feeling rushed. A leisurely approach to dining not only aligns with local customs but also allows you to fully appreciate the cultural significance of the meal.

Engage with Locals: Cartagena's culinary gems are often discovered through the recommendations of locals. Strike up conversations with residents, whether it's your waiter, a fellow diner, or a friendly local you meet on the streets. Colombians are proud of their gastronomic heritage and are often eager to share their favorite eateries and hidden culinary treasures. These personal recommendations can help you enjoy authentic dining experiences that will be very unique and memorable.

Street Food Adventures: Don't shy away from street food; instead, embrace the vibrant world of Cartagena's street-side stalls. Venture into local markets and plazas to sample traditional snacks and bites. From arepas to empanadas, street vendors offer a plethora of flavors that provide a true taste of Colombian street food culture. Ensure that the vendor follows basic hygiene practices, and then indulge in the delicious offerings that capture the essence of Cartagena's culinary diversity.

Cultural Respect: While enjoying your meals, be mindful of cultural respect. Colombians appreciate polite gestures and expressions of gratitude. Simple phrases like "gracias" (thank you) and "por favor" (please) go a long way in showing appreciation for the hospitality you receive. Engaging in local customs, such as the customary greeting of "buen provecho" (enjoy your meal) to fellow diners, adds a touch of cultural courtesy to your dining experience.

Sip on Local Specialties: Explore the world of Colombian beverages by sipping on local specialties. Try traditional aguapanela, a sweetened water made from panela (unrefined cane sugar), or indulge in a cup of freshly brewed Colombian coffee. Experiment with regional fruit juices and refreshing beverages to complement your meals. Embracing local drinks adds a delightful dimension to your culinary adventure.

By incorporating these dining etiquettes and local foodie tips into your Cartagena experience, you'll not only savor the city's flavors but also engage with its cultural heart. Embrace the warmth of Colombian hospitality, explore the streets with a curious palate, and let the local dining customs become an integral part of your gastronomic journey in Cartagena.

CHAPTER 5: THINGS TO DO AND OUTDOOR ACTIVITIES

Embark on a captivating exploration of Cartagena's outdoor wonders, where every activity promises a blend of adventure, relaxation, and the discovery of hidden gems. Dive into the crystal-clear Caribbean waters with snorkeling and water sports, immersing yourself in the vibrant underwater world that surrounds the city. Feel the exhilaration of the sea breeze as you sail through the mangroves, an ecological sanctuary teeming with biodiversity and natural beauty.

For those seeking the ultimate beach bliss, Cartagena offers sandy shores that invite relaxation and recreation. Feel the warm sand beneath your toes and let the rhythmic waves create a soothing melody. Whether it's the lively atmosphere of Bocagrande Beach or the tranquil escape of La Boquilla Beach, each coastal stretch caters to a different mood, making it the perfect setting for a day of sun-soaked rejuvenation.

Venture beyond the beaches and dive into the lush landscapes surrounding Cartagena, where hiking adventures unveil breathtaking views and hidden wonders. Explore trails that lead to elevated vantage points, providing panoramic perspectives of the city's coastal beauty and colonial architecture. The hiking trails offer a perfect blend of exploration and exercise, allowing you to connect with the natural allure that envelops Cartagena.

For those yearning to discover the city's soul away from the well-trodden paths, set out on a journey to uncover hidden gems off the beaten path. Stroll through the colorful streets of Getsemaní, where vibrant street art and local life converge.

Explore the lesser-known corners of the city, where colonial charm meets contemporary creativity. These offbeat discoveries offer a unique perspective, inviting you to connect with Cartagena's authenticity beyond the tourist hotspots.

In Cartagena, outdoor activities transcend the ordinary, offering a kaleidoscope of experiences that cater to every traveler's desires. Whether you're an adventure enthusiast, a beach lover, or a seeker of hidden treasures, the city's outdoor wonders invite you to create memories that resonate with the natural and cultural richness of this Colombian gem.

Snorkeling and Water Sports

Dive into the aquatic wonders surrounding Cartagena by indulging in exhilarating snorkeling and water sports adventures. Head to the Rosario Islands, a pristine archipelago located about 45 minutes by boat from Cartagena's harbor. These islands boast crystal-clear waters and vibrant coral reefs, providing an ideal setting for underwater exploration. Numerous tour operators in Cartagena offer snorkeling excursions to the Rosario Islands, providing you with the opportunity to witness the mesmerizing marine life that inhabits the Caribbean Sea.

One such popular spot for snorkeling is around Isla Grande, the largest of the Rosario Islands. Here, you can glide through the turquoise waters and encounter a kaleidoscope of colorful fish and coral formations. Snorkeling gear is typically provided by tour operators, making it accessible for both beginners and experienced enthusiasts. The underwater spectacle unfolds as you immerse yourself in the warm Caribbean sea, creating an unforgettable experience.

For those seeking a more dynamic water adventure, consider engaging in additional water sports activities available at the Rosario Islands. Jet skiing, paddleboarding, and kayaking are among the options that allow you to interact with the pristine waters in diverse ways. Local guides and instructors are on hand to ensure a safe and enjoyable experience. The thrill of speeding through the waves or calmly paddling across the serene seascape adds an extra layer of excitement to your day in this tropical paradise.

To embark on this aquatic escapade, head to the Muelle de la Bodeguita (Bodeguita Pier) in Cartagena's Old Town. Various tour operators and boat services operate from this pier, offering half-day or full-day snorkeling and water sports packages to the Rosario Islands. As you venture into the turquoise depths, let the beauty of the underwater realm and the excitement of water sports create lasting memories against the backdrop of Cartagena's coastal charm.

Exploring the Mangroves

Embark on a serene and enchanting journey by exploring the mangroves that surround Cartagena, revealing a hidden ecosystem teeming with biodiversity and natural beauty. Located in the La Boquilla area, just a short drive from the city, these mangroves provide a captivating escape into a lush world of winding waterways and thriving plant and animal life.

To immerse yourself in the mangrove experience, consider taking a guided boat tour. Local operators offer excursions that navigate through the intricate network of mangrove tunnels, allowing you to witness the unique flora and fauna that call this coastal ecosystem home. Board a traditional wooden canoe, and let an experienced guide lead you through the narrow channels, providing insights into the mangroves' ecological significance.

As you drift through the mangroves, observe the dense tangle of mangrove roots, which serve as vital habitats for various marine species. Keep an eye out for birdlife, including herons and kingfishers, that find refuge among the branches. The tranquility of the mangrove surroundings offers a stark contrast to the bustling energy of Cartagena, providing a peaceful retreat for nature enthusiasts and those seeking a break from the city's vibrant streets.

Exploring the mangroves is not only an opportunity to connect with nature but also a chance to support local communities. Many tours are operated by locals who possess a deep understanding of the mangroves and their ecological importance. Your visit contributes to sustainable tourism practices that help preserve these vital ecosystems and support the livelihoods of those who call the coastal regions home.

To begin your mangrove adventure, head to La Boquilla and inquire about boat tours at local tour operators or the community's cooperative. With the rustle of the mangrove leaves and the gentle flow of the water guiding your way, this exploration promises a tranquil escape into the heart of Cartagena's natural wonders.

Beach Bliss

Indulge in the epitome of relaxation and coastal charm as you discover the beach bliss that awaits in and around Cartagena. With its sandy shores, turquoise waters, and vibrant atmosphere, Cartagena's beaches offer a perfect escape from the city's hustle and bustle. Whether you seek lively scenes or secluded coves, the beaches in and around Cartagena cater to every beachgoer's preference.

Bocagrande Beach: Situated in the heart of Cartagena, Bocagrande Beach is a lively stretch of golden sand lining the city's modern waterfront. Easily accessible from the Old Town, this beach invites both locals and tourists alike. The long shoreline provides plenty of space to sunbathe and enjoy the Caribbean breeze. Bocagrande's proximity to hotels, restaurants, and shops ensures you can seamlessly transition from beach relaxation to exploring the nearby city amenities.

La Boquilla Beach: For a more serene beach experience, head to La Boquilla Beach, located a short drive from Cartagena. This peaceful haven offers a quieter retreat surrounded by mangroves and the soothing sound of lapping waves. The beach's tranquil ambiance makes it an ideal spot for those seeking a more secluded escape. Local fishermen often dot the shore, providing a glimpse into the authentic coastal lifestyle.

Playa Blanca: If you crave a pristine, postcard-perfect beach day, venture to Playa Blanca, a dazzling stretch of white sand located on Barú Island, accessible by boat or road. The journey itself becomes part of the adventure as you navigate through the scenic landscapes. Playa Blanca's crystal-clear waters and soft sands create an idyllic setting for sunbathing, swimming, and enjoying water sports. Numerous beachside vendors offer refreshing coconut drinks and local snacks, adding to the laid-back beach atmosphere.

Islas del Rosario (Rosario Islands): Escape the mainland entirely and set sail to the Islas del Rosario, a collection of picturesque islands and coral reefs off the coast of Cartagena. These islands boast pristine beaches surrounded by vibrant coral formations, making them a haven for snorkeling and water activities. Day tours to the Rosario Islands often include beach stops, allowing you to bask in the sun, snorkel in the clear waters, and relish the untouched beauty of these tropical paradises.

Turbaco Beach: For a local beach experience that's off the tourist radar, consider Turbaco Beach, located a short drive from Cartagena. This hidden gem offers a tranquil atmosphere and a chance to interact with friendly locals. Surrounded by lush greenery, Turbaco Beach provides a peaceful escape where you can unwind in a more secluded coastal setting.

To access these beach havens, transportation options such as taxis, buses, or organized tours are readily available. Depending on your preference, you can opt for the lively atmosphere of Bocagrande, the tranquility of La Boquilla, the pristine beauty of Playa Blanca and the Rosario Islands, or the local charm of Turbaco Beach. Whether you're in search of vibrant energy or secluded serenity, Cartagena's diverse beaches promise a blissful coastal experience.

Hiking Adventures

Embark on invigorating hiking adventures that unveil the breathtaking landscapes and scenic viewpoints surrounding Cartagena. While the city is renowned for its coastal beauty, its lush hinterlands offer hiking enthusiasts a unique opportunity to explore nature trails and discover panoramic vistas.

One notable hiking destination is the La Popa Hill, which stands as the highest point in Cartagena. Perched at an elevation of 150 meters, La Popa offers sweeping views of the city, the Caribbean Sea, and the surrounding landscapes. The ascent to the summit involves traversing a winding road or stone steps, allowing hikers to witness the gradual reveal of Cartagena's captivating scenery. The historic Convento de la Popa crowns the hill, adding cultural significance to the natural beauty that unfolds during the hike.

Another trail that promises an enriching hiking experience is the Cerro de la Cruz, located within the city's historic Old Town. Ascend the steps to the summit, and you'll be rewarded with an awe-inspiring panorama of Cartagena's colonial architecture juxtaposed against the azure hues of the Caribbean Sea. The hike not only offers a physical challenge but also serves as a cultural exploration, providing glimpses of the city's historic charm.

For those seeking a more immersive nature experience, the Totumo Volcano presents a distinctive hiking adventure. Located approximately 50 kilometers from Cartagena, this dormant volcano is known for its unique feature — a mud bath crater at its summit. The hike to the top is relatively short and unveils views of the surrounding marshlands. Upon reaching the summit, descend into the mud bath for a therapeutic and buoyant experience, creating a memorable finale to your hiking adventure.

To embark on these hiking excursions, consider local tour operators that offer guided trips to La Popa, Cerro de la Cruz, and Totumo Volcano. Whether you're drawn to city views, cultural landmarks, or natural wonders, Cartagena's hiking trails provide an array of options for outdoor enthusiasts seeking to connect with the diverse landscapes that surround this vibrant Colombian city.

Outdoor Adventure Tips and Essentials

Embarking on outdoor adventures in and around Cartagena requires some thoughtful preparation to ensure a seamless and enjoyable experience. Here are some essential tips and recommendations to enhance your outdoor adventures:

1. Sun Protection: The Caribbean sun can be intense, so pack and apply sunscreen with a high SPF to protect your skin. Don't forget to bring a wide-brimmed hat and sunglasses for additional shade and eye protection.

2. Hydration: Stay hydrated, especially in the warm climate of Cartagena. Carry a reusable water bottle and refill it regularly. Consider adding electrolyte tablets to your water to replenish essential minerals lost through sweating during outdoor activities.

3. Comfortable Footwear: Whether you're hiking La Popa Hill, exploring the mangroves, or strolling along the beaches, comfortable footwear is crucial. Choose sturdy walking shoes or sandals with good grip to navigate various terrains comfortably.

4. Lightweight Clothing: Opt for lightweight, breathable clothing to stay cool during your outdoor adventures. Long sleeves and pants can provide additional protection from the sun, especially if you're hiking or spending extended periods outdoors.

5. Insect Repellent: While Cartagena is not known for extreme insect activity, having insect repellent on hand can be beneficial,

especially if you venture into areas with dense vegetation or mangroves.

6. Portable Snacks: Pack some energy-boosting snacks like trail mix, granola bars, or fresh fruits to keep you fueled during your outdoor excursions. This is particularly handy if you're exploring areas where food options may be limited.

7. Waterproof Gear: If you plan to engage in water sports or visit the beaches, consider bringing a waterproof phone case or a dry bag to protect your valuables from splashes or unexpected rain.

8. Navigation Tools: For hiking or exploring off-the-beaten-path areas, carry a map, or download offline maps on your phone. Familiarize yourself with the trails and landmarks to ensure a safe and enjoyable adventure.

9. Camera or Smartphone: Capture the beauty of Cartagena's outdoor landscapes with a camera or smartphone. Whether you're hiking to a viewpoint, snorkeling in the crystal-clear waters, or discovering hidden gems, having a device to document your experiences will allow you to cherish the memories.

10. Local Guided Tours: Consider joining local guided tours for certain activities, such as snorkeling trips or hiking excursions. Local guides not only provide valuable insights into the area's history and ecology but also enhance your safety and overall enjoyment of the experience.

By incorporating these tips and essentials into your outdoor adventure plans, you'll be well-prepared to explore the diverse landscapes and activities that Cartagena and its surrounding areas have to offer.

CHAPTER 6: ART, CULTURE, AND ENTERTAINMENT

Immerse yourself in the vibrant tapestry of Cartagena's art, culture, and entertainment scene, where every corner echoes with the richness of local creativity. Begin your journey by exploring the city's local arts and crafts, where talented artisans weave cultural stories into intricate creations. From the vibrant markets of Getsemaní to the lively streets of the Old Town, discover a kaleidoscope of colors and textures, from handmade textiles to traditional Colombian crafts, showcasing the heart and soul of Cartagena's artistic spirit.

Delve into the city's cultural heritage by stepping into its museums and galleries. Cartagena's history unfolds within the walls of institutions like the Museo de Oro Zenu, home to an impressive collection of pre-Columbian gold artifacts, and the Palacio de la Inquisición, which narrates the city's colonial past. Roam through contemporary galleries in Getsemaní, where local artists showcase their dynamic interpretations of Cartagena's evolving identity, bridging the gap between tradition and modernity.

Cartagena's cultural calendar comes alive with vibrant festivals and events that reflect the city's lively spirit. From the colorful celebrations of the Cartagena Independence Festival to the rhythmic beats of the Cartagena International Music Festival, immerse yourself in the infectious energy of local festivities. The streets transform into stages, inviting you to dance, revel, and embrace the cultural diversity that defines Cartagena's lively calendar.

As the sun sets, Cartagena's nightlife beckons with a blend of traditional rhythms and contemporary beats. Whether you're sipping cocktails in the historic plazas, dancing to salsa and champeta in local clubs, or enjoying live music in the Getsemaní district, the city's nightlife offers a captivating fusion of old and new. Join the locals in the celebration of life, where the nights are as vibrant as the days.

No exploration of Cartagena's cultural landscape is complete without a visit to its bustling local markets. Dive into the sensory delights of Bazurto Market, where the air is infused with the aromas of exotic fruits, spices, and fresh seafood. Indulge in a shopping spree through the streets of Bocagrande or the artisan markets of San Diego, where you can find unique souvenirs and treasures that encapsulate the essence of your Cartagena experience.

In Cartagena, art, culture, and entertainment converge seamlessly, inviting you to not just witness but actively participate in the vibrant rhythm of the city. From the hands of skilled artisans to the beats of local festivals, every moment is an opportunity to connect with the dynamic spirit of Cartagena's cultural tapestry.

Local Arts and Crafts

Venture into the heart of Cartagena's local arts and crafts scene, a vibrant tapestry woven by talented artisans showcasing the city's cultural richness. The artistic journey begins in the lively neighborhood of Getsemaní, where the streets come alive with color and creativity. Wander through the Plaza de la Trinidad, surrounded by a medley of art stalls and vibrant murals, where local artisans display their handmade treasures. From intricately woven mochilas to vibrant paintings depicting the city's soul, this square is a captivating starting point for exploring Cartagena's artisanal heritage.

As you stroll through the narrow streets of Getsemaní, you'll encounter workshops and boutiques where local artists craft unique pieces. The neighborhood's vibrant energy is a testament to its transformation into a hub of contemporary creativity. Head to Calle del Guerrero, known as Cartagena's Art Street, where numerous galleries showcase the works of emerging and established artists. Here, you can engage with the creators, learning about the inspirations behind their pieces and perhaps even witnessing a work in progress.

For an immersive experience in Cartagena's arts and crafts, visit the Portal de los Dulces in the heart of the Old Town. This charming colonial-era arcade, adorned with bougainvillea, is home to a variety of artisanal shops. Explore the offerings of local craftsmen, from handmade jewelry to traditional Colombian hats. The Portal de los Dulces is not just a shopping destination; it's a cultural enclave where the past and present converge, allowing you to engage with Cartagena's artistic legacy.

To reach the vibrant arts and crafts scene in Getsemaní and the Old Town, you can easily walk from various points within Cartagena or take a short taxi ride. The Plaza de la Trinidad in Getsemaní is a central meeting point, while the Portal de los Dulces in the Old Town is conveniently located near popular landmarks like the Clock Tower and the Cathedral. Let the colors, textures, and stories encapsulated in Cartagena's local arts and crafts become tangible memories of your exploration into the city's cultural soul.

Museums and Galleries

Embark on a captivating journey through Cartagena's rich cultural tapestry by exploring its diverse museums and galleries. These institutions not only showcase the city's historical legacy but also provide a window into its contemporary artistic expressions, blending the old and the new in a harmonious narrative.

Museo de Oro Zenu (Gold Museum): Immerse yourself in the pre-Columbian history of Cartagena at the Museo de Oro Zenu. Located in the heart of the Old Town, this museum houses an impressive collection of gold artifacts crafted by the Zenu indigenous people. Delve into the intricate details of ancient goldsmithing techniques and gain insights into the spiritual significance of these treasures. The museum serves as a cultural bridge, connecting the city's present to its indigenous past.

Palacio de la Inquisición (Palace of the Inquisition): Step back in time at the Palacio de la Inquisición, a colonial-era building that once served as the headquarters of the Spanish Inquisition. Located on Plaza de Bolívar, this museum unravels the dark history of the Inquisition in Cartagena through exhibits that include torture devices, historical documents, and artifacts. Explore the grand architecture of the palace and witness the echoes of a bygone era within its walls.

Museo Naval del Caribe (Naval Museum of the Caribbean): Located within the San Francisco Cloister, the Museo Naval del Caribe offers a fascinating journey through the maritime history of Cartagena and the Caribbean. Discover naval artifacts, ship models, and interactive displays that narrate the city's role as a strategic port and naval stronghold. The museum provides a unique perspective on Cartagena's connection to the sea and its historical importance in naval warfare.

Museo de Arte Moderno (Museum of Modern Art): For a glimpse into Cartagena's contemporary art scene, visit the Museo de Arte Moderno in the Getsemaní neighborhood. This dynamic space showcases the works of both local and international artists, presenting a diverse range of artistic expressions. From paintings to sculptures, the museum reflects the city's evolving cultural identity and its place within the global art discourse.

Casa Museo Rafael Núñez (Rafael Núñez Museum House): Explore the former residence of Rafael Núñez, a prominent Colombian political figure and four-time president. Located in the San Diego neighborhood, this museum house provides a glimpse into the life and times of Núñez through preserved rooms, personal belongings, and exhibits. Stroll through the serene garden and immerse yourself in the history of a key figure in Colombian politics.

To reach these cultural havens, many of which are situated in the Old Town or nearby neighborhoods, you can easily navigate the city on foot or use local transportation options. Dive into the narratives presented by these museums and galleries, where each artifact, painting, or sculpture unfolds a unique chapter in the story of Cartagena's rich and diverse heritage.

Festivals and Events

Cartagena pulsates with energy throughout the year, hosting a vibrant tapestry of festivals and events that celebrate its rich cultural heritage and lively spirit. Immerse yourself in the infectious rhythms and joyful atmosphere of these dynamic gatherings, each offering a unique experience that resonates with the city's vibrant soul.

Cartagena Independence Festival: Join the city in a jubilant celebration of its independence during the Cartagena Independence Festival. Held in November, this lively event brings together locals and visitors alike in a festive atmosphere. Parades, traditional dances, and cultural performances fill the streets, showcasing the pride and resilience of Cartagena's community. The festival is a colorful tapestry of history and culture, allowing you to witness the city's spirit come alive.

Hay Festival Cartagena: Literary enthusiasts and thinkers from around the world converge in Cartagena during the Hay Festival, a global celebration of literature and ideas. Held annually in January, this event transforms the city into a hub of intellectual exchange. Attend thought-provoking discussions, book readings, and cultural events that bridge the gap between literature, art, and societal dialogue. The Hay Festival is a testament to Cartagena's role as a cultural epicenter.

Cartagena International Music Festival: Let the enchanting melodies of classical music fill the historic venues of Cartagena during the Cartagena International Music Festival. Held in January, this event attracts renowned musicians and orchestras, turning the city into a stage for classical masterpieces. From intimate chamber concerts to grand performances in historic theaters, the festival offers a harmonious blend of music and architectural beauty.

Cartagena International Film Festival: Film enthusiasts and cinephiles gather for the Cartagena International Film Festival, an annual event that spotlights the best of Colombian and international cinema. Held in March, the festival features film screenings, discussions, and cultural events that celebrate the art of filmmaking. Explore the diverse cinematic landscape while enjoying the picturesque backdrop of Cartagena's Old Town.

Hay Festivalito: In addition to the main Hay Festival, Cartagena hosts the Hay Festivalito, a special edition tailored for children and families. This kid-friendly event, held concurrently with the main festival, introduces young minds to the world of literature, storytelling, and creativity through interactive workshops, storytelling sessions, and artistic activities.

Participating in these festivals and events offers a unique opportunity to engage with Cartagena's cultural heartbeat.

Nightlife and Entertainment

As the sun sets, Cartagena undergoes a captivating transformation, inviting you to experience the city's vibrant nightlife and entertainment scene. From lively salsa beats to contemporary sounds, the nights in Cartagena pulsate with energy, creating an atmosphere that seamlessly blends tradition and modernity.

Historic Plazas and Open-Air Cafés: Begin your evening by soaking in the enchanting ambiance of Cartagena's historic plazas. The Plaza Santo Domingo and Plaza de Bolívar come alive with the melodies of street musicians, creating an inviting atmosphere for a leisurely evening. Enjoy a drink at one of the open-air cafés lining the plazas, where you can relish the colonial charm and observe the city's lively street life.

Salsa and Champeta Clubs: To truly immerse yourself in the rhythm of Cartagena, venture into the city's salsa and champeta clubs. Dance enthusiasts will find a haven in venues like Café Havana, a legendary salsa club where live bands and expert dancers set the stage for a night of lively moves. Champeta, a genre rooted in Afro-Colombian rhythms, comes to life at Bazurto Social Club, where you can groove to the infectious beats and experience the city's unique musical heritage.

Live Music in Getsemaní: Getsemaní, Cartagena's bohemian neighborhood, is a hotbed of live music venues and eclectic entertainment. Explore the vibrant streets and stumble upon intimate bars and cafés hosting local bands and musicians. The neighborhood's artistic energy infuses the night with a sense of discovery, where you might encounter jazz performances, acoustic sets, or even spontaneous street art exhibitions.

Rooftop Bars with Stunning Views: Elevate your nightlife experience by heading to one of Cartagena's rooftop bars. Bask in the panoramic views of the cityscape and the Caribbean Sea while sipping on crafted cocktails. Popular venues like Café del Mar and Alquimico offer a sophisticated setting where you can enjoy the city lights and revel in the cool ocean breeze.

Casino and Entertainment Complexes: If you're feeling lucky or simply want to indulge in a different form of entertainment, Cartagena's casinos offer a glamorous escape. Test your skills at the slot machines or try your hand at classic table games. Some casinos, like the Casino Rio, also host live entertainment events, adding a touch of glamour to your night out.

Navigating Cartagena's nightlife is a sensory journey that takes you through lively streets, pulsating dance floors, and breathtaking vistas.

Local Markets, Shopping, and Souvenirs

Dive into the vibrant tapestry of Cartagena's local markets, where every corner beckons with colors, aromas, and the authentic spirit of Colombian craftsmanship. From traditional souvenirs to contemporary creations, these markets offer a sensory journey through the city's cultural heritage.

Bazurto Market: Brace yourself for a bustling adventure in the heart of Cartagena at Bazurto Market. Located just outside the Old Town, this lively market is a sensory feast where locals converge to buy and sell everything from fresh produce to handmade crafts. Stroll through the vibrant stalls, inhaling the scents of exotic fruits, spices, and freshly caught seafood. Engage with local vendors, sample regional delicacies, and discover unique souvenirs that encapsulate the dynamic essence of Cartagena's daily life.

San Diego Artisan Market: Nestled in the charming San Diego neighborhood, the San Diego Artisan Market is a treasure trove of handmade crafts and local artwork. Wander through the cobblestone streets, where artisans display their creations in open-air stalls. From vibrant paintings to intricately woven textiles, this market offers a curated selection of unique and authentic souvenirs. Engage with the artisans, learn about their creative processes, and take home a piece of Cartagena's artistic soul.

Las Bóvedas (The Vaults): Located within the historic walls of the Old Town, Las Bóvedas is a series of arched chambers that have been transformed into a vibrant shopping arcade. This iconic market is renowned for its array of artisanal goods, including colorful textiles, handcrafted jewelry, and traditional Colombian crafts. Explore the arches, each housing a variety of stalls, and indulge in a shopping spree where history meets contemporary craftsmanship.

Bocagrande Shopping: For those seeking a blend of modernity and shopping convenience, Bocagrande offers a selection of malls and boutiques. The Bocagrande Shopping Center is a popular destination, housing a mix of local and international brands. Explore the air-conditioned spaces for fashion, accessories, and electronics, providing a contrast to the traditional markets and adding a modern touch to your shopping experience.

Plaza de la Aduana: Uncover the charm of Plaza de la Aduana, a historic square in the Old Town that transforms into an artisan market in the evenings. Local vendors gather to showcase their handmade goods, from leather products to traditional Colombian hats. The square itself becomes a cultural hub, hosting live music and cultural events that enhance the shopping experience with a dose of local entertainment.

Navigating these markets is not just a shopping excursion but an immersion into Cartagena's cultural vibrancy. Whether you're bargaining for treasures in the lively Bazurto Market, perusing the artistic creations in San Diego, or exploring the historic arches of Las Bóvedas, each market tells a unique story and offers an opportunity to carry a piece of Cartagena's soul home with you.

CHAPTER 7: 7-DAY ITINERARY IN CARTAGENA

Day 1: Arrival and Old Town Exploration

Morning:
Begin your Cartagena adventure by arriving at Rafael Núñez International Airport. From the airport, take a taxi or shuttle to your chosen accommodation. Settle in and feel the coastal breeze as you step into the magic of Cartagena. For a relaxed start, head to a local café for a traditional Colombian breakfast. Enjoy arepas, empanadas, and a cup of rich Colombian coffee.

Afternoon:
Immerse yourself in the enchanting history of Cartagena by exploring the Old Town. Start at the iconic Clock Tower (Torre del Reloj), a gateway to the historic district. Wander through the charming streets, lined with pastel-colored colonial buildings. Visit Plaza Santo Domingo, a lively square surrounded by cafes and art galleries. Lunch at a local eatery, sampling Caribbean-inspired dishes.

Evening:
As the sun begins to set, head to the historic walls of Cartagena. Enjoy a leisurely stroll along the fortifications and take in breathtaking views of the Caribbean Sea. For dinner, venture to a rooftop restaurant like Café del Mar for a delightful meal with a panoramic backdrop. End the night with a visit to a salsa club in Getsemaní or a quiet drink at a bar in the Old Town.

Day 2: Rosario Islands Escape

Morning:
Embark on a day trip to the Rosario Islands. Begin your morning with a boat ride from Cartagena to this stunning archipelago. Explore the crystal-clear waters, relax on the white sandy beaches, and perhaps indulge in some snorkeling. Enjoy a beachside lunch with fresh seafood and tropical fruits.

Afternoon:
Continue your island escapade, perhaps trying out water sports or simply basking in the sun. Engage in the laid-back atmosphere, surrounded by palm-fringed beaches and turquoise waters. Take a boat ride to Isla Barú for more secluded spots.

Evening:
Return to Cartagena in the late afternoon. Freshen up and unwind at your accommodation. For dinner, choose from the seafood restaurants in Bocagrande or the charming spots in the Old Town. End the day with a leisurely evening walk along the city walls or a nightcap at a beachside bar.

Day 3: Cultural Immersion in Getsemaní

Morning:
Start your day with a hearty breakfast and then venture to Getsemaní, a vibrant neighborhood brimming with street art and local life. Visit Plaza de la Trinidad, the heart of Getsemaní, where you can witness daily life and maybe catch a local event.

Afternoon:
Explore the streets adorned with colorful murals and street art. Visit local shops and boutiques, supporting local artisans. For lunch, indulge in Colombian street food or try a trendy café for a fusion of flavors.

Evening:
As evening falls, Getsemaní comes alive with a distinct energy. Enjoy dinner at a local eatery, savoring the diverse flavors of Colombian cuisine. Don't miss the chance to dance to champeta or salsa tunes at one of the lively bars in the area.

Day 4: Explore La Popa and San Felipe

Morning:
Embark on a morning visit to Convento de la Popa, perched atop the highest point in Cartagena. Take in panoramic views of the city and the sea. Explore the convent's history and architecture.

Afternoon:
Head to Castillo San Felipe de Barajas, a formidable fortress that played a crucial role in the city's defense. Dive into the historical significance of this UNESCO World Heritage site. Afterward, enjoy lunch at a nearby restaurant.

Evening:
For a change of pace, take a leisurely stroll through Manga, a residential neighborhood known for its colonial-era mansions. Capture the sunset at Café del Mar or another scenic spot, followed by dinner at a local restaurant.

Day 5: Beach Day in La Boquilla

Morning:
Start your day with a relaxing morning at La Boquilla Beach. Travel to this coastal gem, known for its tranquil shores and a mix of local and tourist-friendly atmosphere.

Afternoon:
Bask in the sun, take a dip in the Caribbean waters, and enjoy a seafood lunch at one of the beachside restaurants. Try water sports or opt for a boat ride through the mangroves for a unique experience.

Evening:
Return to Cartagena in the late afternoon. Freshen up at your accommodation and then head to Bocagrande for dinner. Choose from the diverse array of restaurants along the waterfront or within the neighborhood.

Day 6: Art and Shopping Extravaganza

Morning:
Embark on a cultural morning by exploring the Museo de Oro Zenu, delving into the fascinating world of pre-Columbian gold artifacts. Afterwards, stroll through Plaza de Bolívar, surrounded by historic buildings and vibrant street life.

Afternoon:
Indulge in a shopping spree in Las Bóvedas, a series of arches within the Old Town known for its artisanal goods and souvenirs. Explore local boutiques and galleries, perhaps finding a unique piece of Cartagena to take home.

Evening:
Venture to the San Diego neighborhood for dinner at one of the area's charming restaurants. Enjoy a relaxing evening surrounded by colonial architecture and lively streets.

Day 7: Relaxing Day and Farewell

Morning:
On your final day, take a leisurely morning to revisit your favorite spots, relax at a local café, or explore any last-minute activities you may have missed.

Afternoon:
Enjoy a farewell lunch at a restaurant with a view, savoring your last moments in Cartagena. Reflect on the memories made during your stay.

Evening:
As the day draws to a close, bid farewell to Cartagena with a stroll along the city walls or a quiet moment at a beachside spot. Cherish the memories of your week-long journey in this captivating Colombian gem.

CHAPTER 8: PRACTICAL INFORMATION AND TIPS

Etiquette and Customs

Immerse yourself in the local culture of Cartagena by embracing its unique etiquette and customs. Understanding and respecting these aspects will enhance your experience and contribute to positive interactions with the warm and welcoming residents.

Greeting Customs: Colombians are known for their friendliness. A customary greeting involves a handshake and direct eye contact. Additionally, a light hug or a kiss on the cheek (air kiss) is common among friends and acquaintances.

Respect for Personal Space: While Colombians are friendly, it's essential to be mindful of personal space. Maintain a comfortable distance during conversations and avoid standing too close.

Politeness in Conversations: Politeness is highly valued in Colombian culture. Use "por favor" (please) and "gracias" (thank you) liberally in your interactions. It's common to address people using titles like "señor" (Mr.) or "señora" (Mrs.) followed by their last name.

Time and Punctuality: Colombian time can be more relaxed compared to some Western cultures. However, it's respectful to be punctual for formal engagements. Social gatherings may have a more flexible start time.

Dress Modestly: While Cartagena has a tropical climate, it's advisable to dress modestly, especially when visiting religious sites. Pack lightweight and breathable clothing, and consider covering shoulders and knees when appropriate.

Dining Etiquette: When dining in a local's home, it's customary to bring a small gift for the host. During meals, it's polite to wait for the host to begin eating before starting your meal. Complimenting the food is a gesture appreciated by hosts.

Tipping Practices: Tipping is customary in restaurants, and a standard tip is around 10% of the bill. Some establishments may include a service charge, so check your bill. Tipping is also common for other services, like taxi rides and guided tours.

Photography Courtesy: Always seek permission before taking photos of people, especially in more intimate settings or markets. Some locals may prefer not to be photographed.

Learn Basic Spanish Phrases: While many locals in Cartagena may speak some English, learning a few basic Spanish phrases can go a long way in fostering positive interactions. Locals appreciate efforts to communicate in their language.

Respect Local Traditions: Cartagena celebrates various festivals and traditions. If you're fortunate to be in the city during such events, join the festivities respectfully. Understanding and appreciating local customs will enrich your cultural experience.

By embracing the customs and etiquette of Cartagena, you not only show respect to the local culture but also create meaningful connections with the people who call this vibrant city home. Enjoy the warmth and hospitality that Cartagena has to offer, and your journey will undoubtedly be enriched by these cultural nuances.

Language and Communication

Cartagena, a city pulsating with cultural diversity, embraces Spanish as its official language. While you may encounter locals who speak some English, especially in tourist areas, having a basic understanding of Spanish phrases can significantly enhance your experience and interactions with the warm-hearted residents.

Spanish Language Usage:
Spanish is the predominant language spoken in Cartagena, and locals appreciate visitors who make an effort to communicate in their native tongue. While some Colombians in Cartagena, particularly those working in the tourism industry, may speak English, the ability to converse in Spanish opens up doors to more authentic and enriching experiences. Learning common phrases for greetings, ordering food, and asking for directions will go a long way in navigating the city.

Language Diversity:
Colombian Spanish has its unique characteristics, influenced by regional accents and cultural nuances. In Cartagena, the Caribbean flavor infuses the language with a distinctive rhythm and vocabulary. Embrace the local expressions and variations you encounter, and don't hesitate to ask for clarification or assistance when needed.

Politeness and Respect:
Politeness is deeply ingrained in Colombian culture, and the language reflects this. When addressing people, using titles such as "señor" (Mr.) or "señora" (Mrs.) followed by their last name is a customary sign of respect. Simple phrases like "por favor"

(please) and "gracias" (thank you) carry significant weight in demonstrating politeness.

Cultural Understanding through Language:
Beyond practical communication, language serves as a cultural bridge. Engaging in conversations with locals in Spanish allows for a deeper understanding of Cartagena's rich heritage and traditions. It fosters a connection that goes beyond the transactional, providing insights into the daily lives and perspectives of those you encounter.

Local Patience and Appreciation:
Colombians are known for their warmth and patience, especially when it comes to language barriers. Locals often appreciate visitors attempting to speak Spanish and may even offer assistance or corrections with a smile. This mutual respect for language differences creates a welcoming environment for cultural exchange.

Language Learning Opportunities:
For those eager to enhance their language skills, Cartagena provides ample opportunities. Language schools and cultural programs cater to visitors seeking formal instruction. Additionally, engaging in casual conversations with locals, whether at markets, cafes, or during cultural events, offers a practical and immersive way to improve your Spanish.

In essence, language in Cartagena is not just a means of communication but a gateway to the city's soul. Embrace the linguistic diversity, savor the nuances of Colombian Spanish, and let the power of words create lasting connections during your exploration of this enchanting Caribbean gem.

Simple Language Phrases to Know

Basic Greetings:
Hello - Hola (oh-la)
Good morning - Buenos días (bway-nos dee-as)
Good afternoon - Buenas tardes (bway-nas tar-des)
Good evening/night - Buenas noches (bway-nas noh-ches)
How are you? - ¿Cómo estás? (koh-moh es-tas?)

Common Courtesies:
Please - Por favor (por fa-vor)
Thank you - Gracias (gra-cias)
You're welcome - De nada (de na-da)
Excuse me - Perdón (per-don)
I'm sorry - Lo siento (lo sien-to)

Introductions:
My name is... - Mi nombre es... (mee nom-bre es...)
Nice to meet you - Mucho gusto (moo-cho goos-to)
What's your name? - ¿Cómo te llamas? (koh-mo te ya-mas?)

Directions:
Where is...? - ¿Dónde está...? (don-de es-ta...?)
Left - Izquierda (eez-kee-er-da)
Right - Derecha (de-re-cha)
Straight ahead - Todo recto (to-do rech-to)

Numbers:
One - Uno (oo-no)
Two - Dos (doss)
Three - Tres (tres)
Four - Cuatro (kwah-tro)
Five - Cinco (seen-ko)

Dining Out:
Menu - Menú (me-noo)
Water - Agua (ah-gwa)
Food - Comida (co-mee-da)
Delicious - Delicioso (de-li-cio-so)
Bill, please - La cuenta, por favor (la kwen-ta, por fa-vor)

Shopping:
How much does this cost? - ¿Cuánto cuesta esto? (kwan-to kwe-sta es-to?)
I would like to buy... - Me gustaría comprar... (me goo-sta-ree-a kom-prar...)
Can I pay with a card? - ¿Puedo pagar con tarjeta? (pwe-do pa-gar kon tar-he-ta?)

Emergencies:
Help! - ¡Ayuda! (a-yu-da)
I need a doctor - Necesito un médico (ne-se-si-to un me-dee-ko)
Where is the hospital? - ¿Dónde está el hospital? (don-de es-ta el os-pee-tal?)

Travel and Transportation:
Where is the bus station? - ¿Dónde está la estación de autobuses? (don-de es-ta la es-ta-syon de ow-to-boo-ses?)
Taxi - Taxi (tak-see)
Airport - Aeropuerto (ay-ero-pwer-to)
Train - Tren (tren)
I need a map - Necesito un mapa (ne-se-si-to un ma-pa)

Weather:
What's the weather like today? - ¿Cómo está el clima hoy? (koh-mo es-ta el klee-ma oy?)
It's hot - Hace calor (ah-se ka-lor)

It's cold - Hace frío (ah-se free-o)
Rain - Lluvia (yoo-via)
Sun - Sol (sol)

Learning these simple phrases will not only help you navigate Cartagena but also make your interactions with locals more enjoyable. Don't be afraid to practice, and remember, locals appreciate the effort!

Health and Safety Tips

Embarking on a journey to Cartagena promises a delightful adventure filled with culture, history, and vibrant experiences. To ensure a safe and enjoyable trip, consider the following health and safety tips:

1. Stay Hydrated:
The Caribbean climate in Cartagena can be warm and humid. Carry a reusable water bottle and stay hydrated, especially if you're exploring outdoor attractions. Drink bottled or purified water to avoid any stomach discomfort.

2. Sun Protection:
The sun can be intense, so protect yourself by wearing sunscreen with a high SPF, a hat, and sunglasses. Reapply sunscreen throughout the day, especially if you're spending extended periods outdoors.

3. Mosquito Prevention:
While the risk of mosquito-borne diseases is relatively low, it's advisable to use insect repellent, particularly if you plan on visiting areas near mangroves or during the evening. Consider wearing long sleeves and pants for added protection.

4. Local Cuisine Precautions:
Indulge in the delicious local cuisine, but exercise caution to prevent food-related issues. Choose reputable eateries, ensure that food is cooked thoroughly, and avoid consuming raw or undercooked seafood.

5. Secure Your Belongings:
Cartagena is generally safe, but like any tourist destination, be mindful of your belongings. Keep valuables secure, use anti-theft bags, and avoid displaying expensive items in crowded places.

6. Transportation Safety:
If using taxis, ensure they are official and use reputable ride-hailing services. Be cautious when crossing streets and adhere to traffic signals. Public transportation, while generally safe, requires vigilance.

7. Emergency Services:
Know the location of the nearest hospital or medical center. The emergency number in Colombia is 123 for police, 132 for an ambulance, and 131 for the fire department.

8. Travel Insurance:
Consider obtaining comprehensive travel insurance that covers medical emergencies, trip cancellations, and lost belongings. Confirm that the policy includes coverage for activities you plan to engage in, such as water sports or adventure excursions.

9. Cultural Respect:
Respect local customs and traditions. Ask for permission before taking photos, especially of people. Dress modestly when visiting religious sites, and be mindful of cultural sensitivities.

10. Language Barrier:
While many locals may understand basic English, having a few essential Spanish phrases can be helpful in emergencies or when seeking assistance. Locals appreciate visitors who make an effort to communicate in their language.

11. Beach Safety:
If enjoying the beaches, swim in designated areas with lifeguards. Pay attention to warning flags, and be cautious of strong currents. Stay hydrated, especially in the sun.

12. Vaccinations:
Ensure your routine vaccinations are up-to-date. Depending on your travel history and planned activities, consult a healthcare professional to determine if additional vaccinations, such as for hepatitis A and typhoid, are recommended.

By incorporating these health and safety tips into your travel plan, you can focus on absorbing the beauty and charm of Cartagena, confident in the knowledge that you are prioritizing your well-being throughout your journey.

Emergency Contacts

During your stay in Cartagena, it's important to be aware of emergency contact numbers for various situations. In case of any unforeseen circumstances, these contacts can provide assistance and support. Here are the essential emergency numbers:

1. Police:
Emergency Number: 123

2. Medical Emergency:
Ambulance: 132

3. Fire Department:
Emergency Number: 131

4. Tourist Police:
Cartagena Tourist Police: +57 5 660 1580

5. U.S. Embassy in Bogotá (for U.S. Citizens):
Address: Calle 24 Bis No. 48-50, Bogotá, D.C., Colombia
Phone: +57 1 2752000
Website: U.S. Embassy Bogotá

6. Hospital and Medical Centers:
Hospital Universitario del Caribe:
Address: Carrera 46 No. 47-15, Cartagena, Colombia
Phone: +57 5 669 9000

Hospital Naval de Cartagena:
Address: Cra. 25 No. 20-10, Cartagena, Colombia
Phone: +57 5 654 5580

Centro Médico Alta Complejidad:
Address: Calle 30 No. 17A-29, Cartagena, Colombia
Phone: +57 5 660 0770

7. Pharmacy (Farmacia) - 24-Hour Pharmacies:
Farmacia Pasteur 24 Horas:
Address: Av. Venezuela #38-68, Cartagena, Colombia
Phone: +57 5 660 8852

Drogas La Rebaja 24 Horas:
Address: Av. Pedro de Heredia #30A-150, Cartagena, Colombia
Phone: +57 5 668 9888

Note: Before your trip, it's advisable to save these numbers in your phone and share them with fellow travelers. Additionally, familiarize yourself with the location of the nearest hospital or medical center to your accommodation. In case of an emergency, always seek professional assistance promptly.

Communication and Internet Access

Staying connected in Cartagena is essential for navigating the city, sharing your travel experiences, and accessing useful information. Here's a guide to communication and internet access:

1. Local SIM Cards:
Consider purchasing a local SIM card upon arrival. Major carriers like Claro, Movistar, and Tigo offer prepaid plans with data, call, and text options. You can find SIM cards at airports, convenience stores, or official carrier outlets.

2. Wi-Fi Hotspots:
Most hotels, restaurants, cafes, and shopping malls in Cartagena provide free Wi-Fi for customers. Confirm the availability and ask for the password when needed. The historic Old Town is well-covered with Wi-Fi, making it convenient for tourists.

3. Internet Cafés:
While internet cafés are less common nowadays, you may still find some in Cartagena. These establishments offer computer access and internet services for a fee. Check with locals or your accommodation for recommendations.

4. Mobile Data:
Mobile data coverage is generally good in Cartagena. Ensure your phone is unlocked before arriving, allowing you to use a local SIM card for data access. This is particularly useful when navigating with maps or using ride-sharing apps.

5. Social Media and Messaging Apps:
Stay connected with friends and family through social media platforms and messaging apps. WhatsApp is widely used in Colombia, and you can easily communicate with locals and fellow travelers.

6. Internet Speeds:
In major tourist areas and commercial districts, you can expect decent internet speeds. However, speeds may vary in more remote locations. Cafés and hotels usually provide reliable connections for basic internet needs.

7. Cybersecurity:
Use virtual private networks (VPNs) for added cybersecurity, especially when connecting to public Wi-Fi networks. This ensures a secure connection, protecting your sensitive data.

8. Language Translation Apps:
Language barriers can be overcome with translation apps. Download a reliable translation app with an offline mode to assist in communication, especially if you're not fluent in Spanish.

9. Emergency Communication:
Save important contact numbers in your phone, including emergency services, your embassy, and local authorities. Having this information readily available ensures a prompt response in case of an emergency.

10. Internet Service Providers:
If you're staying in a rented accommodation for an extended period, inquire about the internet service provider. Some apartments or homes may have dedicated Wi-Fi connections.

By considering these communication tips, you'll be well-equipped to stay connected, share your experiences, and navigate Cartagena with ease. Whether you're exploring the historic streets or enjoying the beaches, staying connected ensures a seamless and enjoyable travel experience.

Useful Apps, Websites, and Maps

Google Maps (www.google.com/maps):
Google Maps is an invaluable tool for navigating the streets of Cartagena. It provides real-time directions, detailed maps, and information about nearby attractions. Ensure you download offline maps to navigate even when you don't have an internet connection.

Uber (www.uber.com):
Uber operates in Cartagena, providing a convenient and often more affordable option for getting around the city. The app allows you to request rides, track your driver, and pay seamlessly through the platform.

iTranslate (www.itranslate.com):
Language barriers can be overcome with iTranslate. This app offers translation services for numerous languages, making it useful for communicating with locals. Download language packs for offline use to assist with communication in areas with limited internet access.

WhatsApp (www.whatsapp.com):
WhatsApp is widely used in Colombia for messaging and calls. Stay connected with friends, family, and fellow travelers. Additionally, many businesses, including tour operators and accommodations, use WhatsApp for communication.

Yelp (www.yelp.com):
Yelp is a valuable resource for discovering local restaurants, cafes, and businesses in Cartagena. Read reviews, view photos, and find recommendations from other travelers to enhance your dining and exploration experiences.

XE Currency Converter (www.xe.com):
For currency conversion, use the XE Currency Converter app. Stay updated on exchange rates to manage your budget effectively. The app works offline, providing convenience when you're exploring areas without internet access.

Cartagena Official Tourism Website (www.cartagenadeindias.travel):
Explore the official tourism website for Cartagena for comprehensive information on attractions, events, and travel tips. This website offers insights into the city's history, culture, and practical advice for tourists.

Waze (www.waze.com):
Waze is a community-driven navigation app that provides real-time traffic updates and optimal routes. It's particularly useful for avoiding traffic jams and finding the quickest paths to your destination in Cartagena.

Colombia Travel (www.colombia.travel):
The Colombia Travel website is a helpful resource for planning your entire Colombian adventure. Explore various destinations, cultural insights, and travel tips to make the most of your time in Cartagena and beyond.

Weather.com (www.weather.com):
Check the weather forecast for Cartagena on Weather.com before planning outdoor activities. The site provides accurate and up-to-date information, helping you prepare for the climate during your visit.

By incorporating these apps, websites, and maps into your Cartagena adventure, you'll have a wealth of information at your fingertips, making your exploration of this vibrant city even more enjoyable and seamless.

CONCLUSION

As we reach the end of this guide, I hope you're as excited about exploring Cartagena as I am passionate about sharing its wonders with you. Cartagena, with its rich history, vibrant culture, and enchanting landscapes, is not just a destination; it's an experience waiting to unfold.

In the heart of the Caribbean, Cartagena's cobblestone streets whisper tales of centuries past. The Old Town, a UNESCO World Heritage site, invites you to wander through its colonial alleys, where every corner unveils a piece of history. From the imposing Castillo San Felipe de Barajas to the lively Plaza Santo Domingo, each step is a journey through time.

But Cartagena is not just about history; it's a city that beats to the rhythm of its people. Engage with locals in the bustling markets, savor the flavors of Colombian cuisine, and lose yourself in the lively beats of Afro-Caribbean music. Getsemaní, with its colorful street art and lively atmosphere, is a testament to the city's contemporary spirit.

The sun-kissed beaches, such as Bocagrande and La Boquilla, offer a perfect escape for relaxation, while the nearby Rosario Islands beckon with crystal-clear waters and underwater wonders. Whether you're a history enthusiast, a foodie, or a beach lover, Cartagena has a piece of paradise waiting just for you.

As you plan your trip, consider the diverse accommodation options, from luxurious hotels with captivating views to cozy stays in the heart of local neighborhoods. Indulge your taste buds in the best restaurants, try local delicacies, and take in the breathtaking views of the city from the historic walls.

Remember to immerse yourself in the local arts, attend festivals, and explore the hidden gems off the beaten path. Dive into the outdoor adventures, from snorkeling in vibrant coral reefs to hiking through lush mangroves. The options are as diverse as the city itself.

Before you embark on your Cartagena adventure, ensure you've considered practicalities like language nuances, transportation choices, and health and safety tips. Familiarize yourself with useful apps, websites, and maps to enhance your journey and stay connected.

So, dear traveler, get ready to step into a world where every street, every smile, and every wave crashing on the shores tells a unique story. Cartagena is not just a destination; it's an emotion, a melody waiting to be heard, a canvas waiting to be painted by your experiences.

Pack your bags, embrace the warmth of Cartagena's sun, let the Caribbean breeze guide your exploration, and get ready to create memories that will linger in your heart long after you bid farewell to this captivating city. Your Cartagena adventure awaits – let the journey begin!

Manufactured by Amazon.ca
Bolton, ON

46072494R00072